THE GERMAN ELEMENT

IN THE

WAR OF AMERICAN INDEPENDENCE

BY

GEORGE WASHINGTON GREENE, LL. D.

NON-RESIDENT PROFESSOR OF AMERICAN HISTORY IN CORNELL
UNIVERSITY, AUTHOR OF "THE LIFE OF MAJOR-GENERAL
NATHANAEL GREENE," "HISTORICAL VIEW OF
THE AMERICAN REVOLUTION," ETC., ETC.

NEW YORK
PUBLISHED BY HURD AND HOUGHTON
Cambridge: The Riverside Press
1876

To

THE HON. WILLIAM GREENE,

OF WARWICK, R. I.

MY DEAR KINSMAN, — I dedicate this volume to you, in order to have the opportunity of publicly reminding you that one so profoundly versed in the unwritten history of his country ought not to withhold his treasures from his countrymen.

  Believe me ever
    Your friend and kinsman,
      GEORGE W. GREENE.

PREFACE.

THE following pages make no pretension to original research. They are founded on the admirable monographs of Doctor Friedrich Kapp, for many years an honored member of the New York bar and now an active member of the Imperial Assembly of his native Germany. During his residence in the United States, Doctor Kapp made special studies in the history of the Germans in America, and especially of those whose names have passed into American history. The result was the lives of Steuben and Kalb, and the history of those unfortunate men whose blood was shed to gratify the avarice of their sovereign; one of the darkest chapters in the history of wicked rulers. From these sources I have drawn freely in preparing this new tribute to the history of my country.

The history of the American war of independence has not yet taken the place which belongs
to it in historical literature.   Its causes, its actors, and its events invest it with an interest for
the statesman, for the philosopher, and for the
lover of picturesque narrative which has never
been surpassed.   It is a great prose epic, with
heroes whom we can love and revere, whose marvelous truths exceed the boldest inventions of
fiction.

In the first decade of the present century one
of the most attractive saloons of Paris was the
saloon of a lady whom, out of reverence for the
memory of her father, Italians loved to call Ma-
dame Beccaria, although she was already the
mother of Alessandro Manzoni.   The conversation of authors and artists — for it was chiefly of
these that the assembly was composed — naturally turned upon literature; and one evening the
question arose, which of all the events of modern
history was best adapted to epic poetry.   The
discussion was long and animated, the French
Revolution and the Thirty Years' War finding
eloquent advocates.   At last, after weighing the
matter deliberately and looking at it from every

point of view, it was unanimously decided that the American war of independence was the fittest of all. In that group of eminent men and women was Carlo Botta, a young Canavese, already tried by persecution in his own Italy, and an eloquent defender of the purity of his native tongue. Following up the train of thought which the evening's conversation had awakened, he took his way homeward through that square so deeply stained with the blood of the victims of the Reign of Terror, and, as he paused on the spot where the guillotine had stood, said to himself: —

"If it be a good subject for an epic poem, why not for a history? It is, and I will write it."

The very next morning he began his studies, and in 1809 gave his great classic to the world.

Shall I complete the story?

The publishers of Italy republished it to their great emolument, while the author, unrecognized by those laws which recognize every other product of labor as the property of the producer, was compelled to sell the last six hundred copies of his own edition to a druggist, at the price of waste paper, in order to purchase for his wife the privilege of dying in her native land.

GEORGE W. GREENE.

WINDMILL COTTAGE, EAST GREENWICH, R. I.
October, 1875.

CONTENTS.

————

BARON VON STEUBEN.

—⋄—

O mostri almen ch'alla virtù latina,
O nulla manca o sol la disciplina.
Or show at least that to Latin virtue, or nothing is wanting
or discipline alone.

. TASSO, Ger. Lib.

BARON VON STEUBEN.

THE name which, passing through the variations of Stoebe, Steube, and Stoeben, finally took its place in modern history under the form of Von Steuben, first appears in the thirteenth century in the list of noblemen who held feudal manors and estates as vassals of Mansfield and Magdeburg. Like the other nobles of the part of Germany to which they belonged, they became Protestants from the beginning of the Reformation, and like the rest of the minor nobility grew poor by the changes introduced into the system of warfare, while the territorial princes grew rich by the confiscation of church property. During the Thirty Years' War, the branch from which the general descended was separated from the parent stock, and won distinction through its successive generations by the pen and the sword. One among them, his grandfather, an eminent theologian, was known by an "able commentary on the New Testament and the Apocalypse." Another, his father's elder brother, was distinguished as a mathematician, a writer upon military science, and the inventor of a new system of fortification. His father, Wilhelm Augustine, was educated at Halle with his two elder brothers, entered the military service of Prussia at the age of sixteen, was married at thirty-one, when a captain of engineers, and, after having served with distinction in the great wars of the century and filled positions of confidence, and trust under Frederick the Great, died in honorable poverty at the age of eighty-four, on the 26th of April, 1783.

Of his ten children, only three, two sons and a daughter, lived to grow up; and of these the subject of our history, Frederick William Augustus Henry Ferdinand, was the eldest. At the time of his birth, November 15, 1730, his father was stationed at the fortress of Magdeburg on the Elbe, and while he was yet a child he followed him, as the duties of service called him, to Cronstadt and the Crimea. When the father returned to Prussia, the son was barely ten years old. Thus all the associations of his infancy and childhood were military: guns, drums, trumpets, forifications, drills, and parades. Before he was fully turned of fourteen another chapter was added to his rude experience: he served under his father as a volunteer in the campaign of 1744, and shared the perils and hardships of the long and bloody siege of Prague.

Fortunately his father, who had received a good education himself, felt the importance of giving the best that he could command to his son. And fortunately, too, the Jesuits' colleges of Neisse and Breslau afforded the means of thorough elementary instruction. Here young Steuben laid the foundations of a superior knowledge of mathematics and acquired a tincture of history and polite literature. And here also he formed an idea of the importance of intellectual ulture, which led him, when first called into active life, to turn to account every opportunity of adding to his store.

About his profession there could be no doubt. even if all his early impressions had not filled him with aspirations for military glory, there could have been no question about the surest road to distinction under Frederick the Great. At seventeen he entered the army as a cadet. In two years he became an ensign; in four more, a lieutenant, and first lieutenant just a year before the breaking out of the Seven Years' War. Of this period two letters are the only words of his own that have been preserved, and those words are in bad French. But the thoughts are those of an ardent young man who knew his profession and loved it, and asked nothing from fortune but a chance to distinguish himself. "Yes, my dear Henry, if there is a war, I promise you at the end of a second campaign that your friend will be either in Hades or at the head of a regiment."

And soon the war came, the great Seven Years' War; not indeed a war of principles and ideas, a political war merely, yet in military science the connecting link between the great wars of Eugene and Marlborough and the development of strategy by Napoleon. Steuben's part in this war was neither a prominent nor a brilliant one. The first campaign found him a first lieutenant; the last left him a major and in temporary command of a regiment. He was wounded at the battle of Prague in May, 1757, and shared the triumph of Rossbach in November, 1757. The next year gave him a wider field. The brilliant, dashing, dare-devil hero of this war was the General von Mayr, an uneducated, self-made soldier, the illegitimate son of a nobleman, one of those men whom war raises to rank and fortune, and peace sends to the jail or the gallows. Forced into the army by necessity he had resolutely made his way to a command, fighting with equal desperation under different banners, and entering at last the Prussian service in season to take an important part in the Seven Years' War. Frederick, who wanted just such a man to oppose to the leaders of the enemy's Croats and Pandours, put him at the head of a free corps, where his dauntless courage and enterprising genius had full play.

Steuben became his adjutant-general and followed him through his brilliant campaign of 1758. At the beginning of 1759, death, which had so often passed the bold adventurer by in the field, came to him in his tent; and then Steuben returned to his regiment, with a knowledge of the management of light infantry and a habit of cool and prompt decision in the tumult of battle which he could hardly have learned so soon or so well in any other school.

He was soon appointed adjutant to General von Hülsen, fought under him in the unsuccessful battle of Kay, in July, was wounded in the murderous battle of Kunersdorf, where Frederick commanded in person, and having, somewhat like Mélas at Marengo, won a victory and prepared his bulletins, was defeated with terrible slaughter on the same day and by the same enemy. Then for two years, from August, 1759, to September, 1761, we lose sight of him. But that he passed them in good service is evident from his reappearance as aid to General Knoblauch when Platen made his brilliant march into Poland against the Prussian rear. And here for a moment the names of father and son appear together, for the elder Steuben, as major of engineers, built the bridge over the Wartha, which the younger Steuben crossed; too swiftly perhaps to clasp his father's hand or do more than exchange a hurried glance of recognition as the headlong torrent of war swept him onward. Some skillful marching came next, with overwhelming odds to make head against, and the scene closes for a time with a blockade and a capitulation: a blockade in an open town desperately defended till ammunition and provisions failed and half the town was on fire, and an honorable capitulation with flying colors and beating drums and all the honors of war.

In this surrender Steuben was the negotiator, and by its terms he followed his general and brother officers to St. Petersburg as prisoner of war. But the imprisonment was a pleasant one, for the Grand Duke Peter, a warm admirer of Frederick, took him into special favor; and it proved, in the end, a surer path to promotion than active participation in a victory, for he did his king such good service with the grand duke that on his return to Prussia he was made captain, and raised from the staff of a subordinate general to that of the great commander himself. And here his military education received its highest finish; for besides what he learnt in the daily performance of his duty under the king's own eye, he was admitted to the lessons upon the higher principles of the art of war which Frederick himself gave to a limited number of young officers, whom he had selected, not for birth or fortune, but for talent and zeal. And thus it was as aid to the king that he took part in the siege of Schweidnitz, and saw the curtain fall upon the checkered scenes of this long and bloody war. The king, well pleased with his services, bestowed upon him a lay benefice with an income of four hundred thalers.

Peace came, and with it an unsparing reduction of the army. " Lieutenant Blücher may go to the devil " was the expressive phrase with which the future marshal was sent back to private life ; and among the reasons assigned for Steuben's withdrawal from the army is dissatisfaction with the new position assigned him in it. However this may be, we find him, soon after the peace of Hubertsburg, traveling for amusement, staying a short time at Halle and Dessau, then going to Hamburg, where he made an acquaintance that was to exercise a decisive influence upon his future career at a decisive moment, the acquaintance of the Count St. Germain ; and last to the baths of Wildbad in Suabia, where he was presented to the Prince of Hohenzollern Hechingen, and, through the influence of the Princess of Würtemberg and Prince Henry of Prussia, received the appointment of grand marshal of his court. An honorable appointment, indeed, but dull work, one would think, for a soldier in the flower of his age. From infancy, with one brief exception, Steuben had known no life but that of for-

tress and camp; had been accustomed to be up
before day and measure his time by drum-beat and
trumpet.   He had been constantly moving to and
fro with his life in his hand, subject to the chances
of a hair's-breadth more or a hair's-breadth less,
in the line of a musket-bullet or cannon-ball.
He had often seen men whom he had messed
with in the morning lying around him at night
wounded, or dying, or dead.   And now he was to
lay him down calmly under a gilded canopy,
sleep softly on down, and let the summer and
winter sun outstrip him in their rising.   His
companions were to be men who spoke in whis-
pers, and bowed long and low; his duties, the
ushering in and out the presence chamber those
of higher rank, and seeing that those of lower
rank were duly attended, each in his degree;
stifling intrigues, allaying discontents, composing
discords; watching over the details of a great
household — for a court is nothing more — and
giving them an air of dignity by personal gravity
and official decorum.

Steuben's character was passing into a new
phase, revealing, as such transitions always do,
qualities hitherto unknown to their possessor or
those who knew him best.   He had had little
time for the dreams of youth.   Life for him had
been full of stern realities.   His only ambition,
the thirst of military glory, had been imperfectly

gratified. He had not won a regiment in two
years, as he had promised his friend Henry that
he would, but neither had he gone to Hades;
and to have been an aid and a chosen pupil of
Frederick was something to dwell upon with satisfaction, even though it left him with but four hundred thalers over his captain's pay. How small
the prospects of advancement in peace time were,
his father's example showed him: a veteran of
forty-seven years' service, without a blot on his
escutcheon, and still only a major of engineers.
And meditating upon these things he could lay
down his sword without regret; and bid farewell
to all the habits and associations of all his life.

But why, in place of that keen, stout sword,
with its plain leather scabbard and plain brass
guard familiar to a soldier's hand, take up the
flimsy blade fit only to rest idly on a courtier's
thigh or be crossed with some other flimsy blade
in a courtier's quarrel? Rest, rest, rest — Steuben
was weary and wanted rest. Far down in the
depths of his nature, but overlaid hitherto and
hidden by the necessities of his position, lay a
love of ease, a longing for social life and the
pleasures of refined intercourse. But that ease, to
satisfy the old soldier's ideas of form and hierarchic
subordination, must be accompanied by dignity;
that repose, to satisfy the old soldier's habits of
daily occupation, must wear a semblance of ac-

tivity.   And where were these to be found in such
happy combination as in the cyclic frivolities of a
petty German court, wherein the daily trifles of
life were performed with all the pompous cere-
monial of a great empire?

And thus, too, we find the measure of Steuben's
political sentiments at this pausing point in his career.   Frederick had burnt his " Antimachiavel "
years before, and reigned like a voluntary dis-
ciple of the eighteenth chapter of the " Prince."
To the common eye thrones were never firmer.
The " Contrat Social " had but just come forth
from the fervid brain of Jean Jacques.   The " Let-
tres Persanes " and " Esprit des Loix " were doing
their work surely but in apparent silence.   Few
shared the Cardinal Fleury's dread of an approaching end of the world.[1]   But Frederick, who protected the French Raynal and frowned on his own
Germans when they ventured to treat profoundly
some of the subjects of the superficial abbé's dec-
lamations, was not the man to encourage the study
of Rousseau or Montesquieu in his camp, and the
camp had been Steuben's world.   Personally independent and possessing an almost exaggerated

---

[1] Unless Cowper's —

> " World that seems
> To toll the death-bell of its own decree,
> And by the voice of all its elements
> To preach the general doom,"

is to be classed with Fleury's prognostics.

sense of dignity, he was still accustomed to call
a king his master and look upon the distinctions
of rank in civil life as he looked upon them in
military life. The rights of the people, the duties
of rulers, the true sources of authority, were questions that he had not yet found leisure to discuss,
and when the leisure came, there was nothing in
his surroundings to invite the discussion. As
grand marshal of the court of a German prince
he found little in his new surroundings to enlarge
the conceptions of the rights of humanity which
he had formed in the army of a German king.

In the busy idleness of the petty court Steuben
passed nearly ten years; acceptable to the prince
for his intelligent zeal and strict performance
of his duty, acceptable to courtiers for the digni-
fied amenity of his manners and the justice of his
dealings. He had leisure for reading, of which
he had once been fond, and for society, in which
he was well fitted to shine. The prince loved
traveling, and Steuben traveled with him when-
ever he went to other courts of Germany, and,
welcomest duty of all, to Paris, where his rank
opened for him the doors of the most celebrated
saloons and procured him the acquaintance of the
men he most desired to know. So contented was
he with this mode of life that he purchased a small
country-seat by the name of Weilheim; and thus,
but for that[1] " vice of courts " which has ever

---

[1] *Inf.* xiii. 62: " Morte comune e delle corti vizio."

reigned in them supreme, he might have floated pleasantly on the easy tide to the French Revolution, and drawn his sword once more with comrades of the Seven Years' War under the banners of the Duke of Brunswick.

But Steuben was a Protestant, the descendant of Protestants from Luther's day downwards; the court was Roman Catholic, and with priests about it who found it hard that a heretic should stand so high and live so intimately with their sovereign. How they intrigued against him, and how cunningly they strove to sow dissensions betwixt the prince and his grand marshal, we can readily conceive, although the story has not come down to us in all its details. But Steuben, well knowing that whatever the immediate result of the actual contest might be, there could be no return to the tranquillity which had formed the chief charm of his position, discreetly bowed to the blast and resigned; carrying with him into private life the esteem of the prince and the friendship of many eminent men whose friendship he had won under the prince's auspices.

Once more a free man, he seems to have experienced some return of military ambition. For a moment there was a prospect of war, and could he have obtained without much effort the rank he felt himself entitled to, he would have entered the service of the emperor. But his heart was so little in the change that he neglected even to present himself to Joseph, as his friend the Prince de Ligne and General Ried had urged him to do, and the negotiations which he had indolently begun were suffered to fall through. In 1769 the Margrave of Baden had conferred upon him the cross of the order of " la Fidélité ; " and now, on resigning his grand marshalship, he first turned his steps towards Carlsruhe, the seat of the margrave's court. Even quieter than that of Hechingen was the life that he led here. Absolute master of his time and of a competent income, he could go whither he would, still sure of meeting or making friends wherever he went. A visit to the country-seat of the Baron von Waldener, in Alsace, brought him once more into contact with the Count St. Germain; and in the winter of 1776, while Washington was struggling through the Jerseys and striking his daring blow at the German mercenaries in Trenton, Steuben was making at Montpellier the acquaintance of the Earl Warwick and Earl Spencer. So intimate did they become that he resolved to extend his circle of travel and make them a visit in England. ·

Paris lay in his way, and as the Count St. Germain had recently been made minister of war, he could not resist the temptation of passing a few days there and congratulating him on his advancement. It was early in May, 1777. Frank-

lin had already taken up his residence at Passy,
and was drawing young and old around him.
Silas Deane had been in France almost a year.
Arthur Lee was there too, busy, active, jealous,
suspicious.   Beaumarchais was gliding to and
fro, as adroit, keen-eyed, and subtle as his own
Figaro.   Paris was unconsciously vibrating to
the touch of the lightning-tamer, and preparing to
hail him as the breaker of misused sceptres.

But it was not of this that Steuben was
thinking as he reëntered Paris on the 2d of May,
but of the new war minister with whom he
had talked of Prussian tactics at Hamburg and
in Alsatia, and of the gay saloons he had been
so much at home in when he visited them with
the Prince of Hechingen.   He would just glance
at them now, just go out to Versailles and tell
the count how glad he was to see him in the
right place, and then cross over into England
and see what kind of a life English noblemen led
in their own castles.   And as soon as he had made
himself comfortable at his hotel, he wrote to tell
the count of his arrival and that he should wait
upon him at an early day.

 " Do not come to Versailles," was the answer.
" In three days I will see you at the arsenal and
will send an officer to conduct you thither.   We
have important questions to discuss together."
And still pondering on this sphinx-like reply, he

saw the three days pass by and the officer come, and found himself once more in the presence of his friend.

Then for the first time, perhaps, certainly for the first time with any approach to personal interest, he heard the story of the revolted colonies, of their perils and their resources, of the sympathy which France and Spain felt for them, and of the danger that with all their courage and resolution, with all the secret aid of their European friends, they might still fail for want of a man like him to organize and discipline their citizen soldiers. Here was glory, here was fortune, here was a field (and St. Germain laid his hand upon the map of America as he spoke), such as no European war could afford, for applying the lessons of his great• master and demonstrating the superiority of the system which they both believed in so firmly.

Steuben was taken by surprise. In all his guesses at the meaning of St. Germain's letter, he had never thought of this. At first the difficulties and objections rose before him in formidable array. St. Germain answered him at length, trying to meet them all. " What would you advise me, not as a minister but as a friend ? " " Sir, as a minister I have no advice to give you on these subjects ; but as your friend I would never advise you to do anything which I would not do myself were I not employed in the king's service."

Thus ended the first interview, and Steuben went thoughtfully down the old stairway which Sully and France's best king but one had often trod together, when the America that he had been asked to go and fight for was a wilderness. Next day they met again. Twenty-four hours' reflection had removed some doubts, awakened some hopes. It was but a distant sound of the trumpet, but the old spirit — the spirit formed in infancy, cherished through boyhood, and accepted in manhood as the chief spring of action — was stirred again. It may be, too, that a still deeper cord had been touched, and that he felt it would be a generous as well as a glorious thing to fight on the side of a republic contending for her liberty. But liberty was a word not yet familiar to his lips. Glory had its meaning and rank its value. Could he be sure of winning them?

With many warnings to be cautious, to keep away from Versailles and not allow himself to be too freely seen in Paris, St. Germain gave him a letter to Beaumarchais; Beaumarchais introduced him to Deane; Deane took him to Franklin. Thus they stood face to face, the philosopher-diplomatist with his Quaker-cut drab, and the soldier-courtier with the glittering star of the order of " Fidélité " on his breast; the eye that had been

trained to look closely into the phenomena of
nature, and read the workings of the heart in the
play of the features, looking straight into the eye
that had been trained to look into the cannon's
mouth and detect the signs of success or disaster
in the wild tumult of battle. " This is no en-
thusiast," Franklin must have said to himself as
he scanned the sun-embrowned face, the strong
features, the well-rounded forehead, the bushy
eyebrows, uplifted as if the clear orbs they shaded
were ever on the watch, the large nose not wholly
Roman but very near it, the full lower lip sug-
gestive of good cheer fully appreciated, and the
projecting chin, all borne with the upright precision of a man who had worn a uniform from his
childhood. " No young Marquis de Lafayette this,
fresh from the schools, with romantic dreams of
liberty and human virtue. Here is a sword to
sell, perhaps something more ; but what are
swords good for but to cut men to pieces ? and it
is rather hard that I, who have passed over fifty
of my seventy-one years in trying to teach men
how to take care of themselves and convince them
that they are never so happy as when they live
like brothers — I, who have often said that I never
knew a bad peace or a good war, should in my old
age become a sharpener of swords and swords-
men." " A strange way this, of persuading men
to come and shed their blood for you," thought

Steuben as he listened incredulously to the suggestion of some grant of a couple of thousand acres of land as a compensation for his services, and with something very like indignation when Franklin told him with " a manner to which he was then little accustomed " (not the court manner, that is, but one that he became well accustomed to in the sequel) " that he had no authority to enter into engagements and could not advance him anything for the expense of his voyage."

His blood was roused.   This was not the way to speak to a man whom the great king had honored with his confidence, and in the heat of his anger away he went to Beaumarchais, to say that he should go immediately back to Germany and did not want to hear anything more about America.   Next day he went to Versailles.   St. Germain seemed hurt at his decision, but whatever his knowledge of other men may have been, he knew Steuben thoroughly ; and instead of breaking with him he invited him to pass a few days at his house.   This at least Steuben could not refuse.   After dinner the Spanish Embassador, Count Aranda, came in ; not, perhaps, altogether by accident.   " Here is a man," said St. Germain as he presented Steuben to him, " who will risk nothing, consequently he will gain nothing."

When Steuben formed at Montpellier the acquaintance of Earl Spencer and the Earl of Warwick, he formed at the same time the acquaintance of the Prince de Montbarey, who like most of the men of distinction whom he was brought into connection with, conceived a high opinion of his talents and an affection for his person. He too was at Versailles, and Steuben, as St. Germain had doubtless foreseen, went to wait upon him. Another sharp attack upon his resolution by another friend. "I can determine nothing," he said, "until I return to Germany." But the idea had taken possession of his mind, and his friends must have felt almost sure of him when they saw him turn his steps homeward instead of going to England.

It has taken us but three pages to tell this story, but it took three months to act it in, and July was near its end when Steuben reached Rastadt. A letter from Beaumarchais was there before him, telling him that a ship and money were ready for him and that Count St. Germain expected his immediate return. A letter from the count himself urged him to hasten back to Versailles. Here, as with Deane, Beaumarchais was evidently acting as the agent of the ministry, and acting in a manner worthy of the author of the "Mariage de Figaro" and the "Mémoire à Consulter." How could a straightforward, hot-blooded, honor-loving Steuben hope to break through the toils which such a hand had spread?

Just at that time the Prince Louis William of Baden was at Rastadt, and Steuben, who placed great confidence in his judgment, told him the story and showed him the letters. Prince Louis, himself a lieutenant-general in the service of Holland, could see no room for hesitation, and thus between two princes, three counts, and the adroitest of negotiators, the aid-de-camp of the most absolute of kings surrendered himself to the service of the most democratic of republics.

There were still difficult details to arrange. First, Frederick's consent to transfer to Steuben's nephew, the Baron von Canitz, his canonry of Havelberg which now brought him an income of four thousand six hundred livres. Then the fixing upon a definite character to present himself in, and securing, as far as possible, the means of making his application to Congress successful.

It was already known in France that a strong feeling had been excited in America by the facility with which the Congress had given commissions to foreign officers. On the very day that Steuben returned to Paris to resume his negotiations, Washington, from the camp in which he was watching the movements of Sir William Howe, wrote to Franklin " that every new arrival was only a new source of embarrassment to himself, and of disappointment and chagrin to the

gentlemen who came over." [1] It was evident
that no Major, no Colonel Steuben could be advanced to a position in which he could introduce
the reforms which the French minister felt it to
be so important to effect, without seriously offend-
ing the just susceptibilities of the native officers.
The refusal to confirm Deane's contract with Du
Coudray was one of the objections which Steuben
had urged after his interview with Franklin.
And yet St. Germain and Vergennes were both
convinced that without a reform in the organization of the American army, the money and stores
of France would be given in vain.

It was decided, therefore, that Steuben should
assume the rank of a lieutenant-general, an assumption imperfectly borne out by his actual
rank of General of the Circle of Suabia; and to
meet the objection that the American agents had
no authority to treat with him, that he should
merely wait upon them to announce his intention
of serving one or two campaigns as a volunteer,
and ask letters to the leading members of Congress.

He had not yet seen Vergennes. On the third
day after his return Montbarey introduced him
to the minister in a special audience. " You are
determined, then, to go to America," said the veteran diplomatist.

---

[1] Sparks, *Writings of Washington*, v. 33.

"Do you think the idea extravagant?" asked Steuben. "On the contrary, it is the road to fame and distinction; but I strongly recommend you to make an agreement beforehand, and not rely too implicitly on republican generosity."

Steuben replied that he should make no conditions; but that if the republic should prove ungrateful he was sure that the King of France would not, and that Count Vergennes and the Prince de Montbarey would take care that his services should not go unrewarded. The minister was instantly on his guard. "You know very well that it is impossible for us to make conditions with you. I can only say to you, Go, succeed, and you will never regret the step you have taken."

His preparations were now made rapidly. With St. Germain he discussed the reforms he proposed to introduce into the American army. From Beaumarchais he received as a loan the money for his outfit and passage. He chose four officers for aids, De l'Enfant, De Romanai, Des Epinières, and De Ponthière. Not knowing English he required a secretary and interpreter, and at Beaumarchais' house he found Peter S. Duponceau, well known some thirty years ago to the citizens of Philadelphia as a hale old man, to the legal world as a skillful lawyer, to publicists as the translator of Bynkershoeck, to the world of letters as the author of a treatise on the

Chinese language which won the prize of the Institute of his native France ; but then a gay, lighthearted young Frenchman of seventeen, with a remarkable talent for the study of language, and a premonitory passion for English which won him, at the Benedictine convent where he studied, the nickname of L'Anglais.   Two vessels were upon the point of sailing for America with part of the arms and stores furnished by Beaumarchais under the name of Hortalez & Co., and the royal commissioner gave Steuben his choice of the two. By the advice of Count Miranda he fixed upon the Heureux, a twenty-four gun ship which was to sail from Marseilles under the name of Le Flamand.   Steuben, also, assumed a new name, Frank, and as a protection in case of capture by the English, received dispatches under that name to the governor of Martinique.   Then, cheerful, self-reliant, nothing doubting but that two or three years would see him safely returned with a full purse and laureled brow, to talk over his campaigns in the saloons of Paris and at the watering-places of Germany, he embarked with his military family on the 26th of September, 1777, just fifteen days after the battle of Brandy-wine, and while the weary and half-trained band which before another campaign he was to form into a disciplined army was slowly making its way to the position from whence, in eight days more, it was to make its bold dash upon Germantown.

The Flamand's passage was long, boisterous, and perilous; first down the Mediterranean, along the bold, mountainous coast of Spain, and then, with Africa slowly receding on the left and Spain on the right, and sailing unconsciously over Trafalgar, Steuben took his last look of the Old World with its memories, and stretched boldly out into the Atlantic, on the path of a New World and its hopes.

He was familiar with the monotony of a camp, and found it no bad preparation for the monotony of a ship. To while away the time he amused himself with mathematical calculations, shot at a mark with his companions, read the Abbé Raynal, kindling the hitherto dormant fires of republicanism, and doubtless also often thought long and deeply on the best methods of applying Prussian tactics to an army of freemen. More than once, too, the monotony was broken. A severe gale off the coast of Africa may have awakened unpleasant thoughts of slavery among the Moors. Another, off the coast of Nova Scotia, gave him a foretaste of American winds in November. There were seventeen hundred-weight of gunpowder on board, and the forecastle was three times on fire. There were some gunpowder spirits on board, also, who stirred up a mutiny which was only put down by hard fighting, fourteen against eighty-four. At last the land came in sight, and on a bright, clear,

1st of December the Flamand entered the harbor of Portsmouth, New Hampshire, and Steuben saw for the first time the flag of the republic waving over an American fortress.

Assuming at once the dignity of his rank, he sent Duponceau ashore to announce his arrival to the American commander. And then the waggish youngster, in his scarlet regimentals turned up with blue, won the bet he had made on the passage, that he would kiss the first girl he saw. For walking up to one, as none but a Frenchman could, he told her that he was come to fight the battles of her country, and that before he left his own he had solemnly vowed to ask, as a token of success, a kiss from the first lady he met. The damsel listened, and moved either by a sense of patriotism, or by reverence for the sanctity of a vow, or by the eloquence of young eyes and a fresh uniform, or because she did not disapprove of kissing, held with a becoming blush her cheek or her lips — the record does not say which — to the adventurous salute.

As soon as General Langdon learned that the anchoring ship held a Prussian lieutenant-general, a veteran of the Seven Years' War, he hastened on board to welcome him, and, taking him and his suite in his barge, brought them to the landing, whither the whole town was flocking to gaze at and greet them. Meanwhile the guns of the fortress fired a lieutenant-general's salute, and the ships in the harbor, displaying their flags, joined in the national welcome. At that day's dinner Steuben first heard of the surrender of Burgoyne, and hailed the tidings as a happy omen. The day following he visited the fortifications, and the next reviewed the troops. One of his earliest cares, also, was to write to Washington and Congress, expressing his " desire " to deserve the title of a citizen of America by fighting for her liberty. With his own letters he forwarded copies of those of Franklin, Deane, and Beaumarchais. Then, on the 12th of December, he set out for Boston.

Here his chief entertainer was John Hancock, who was just returning to private life after honorable service in Congress; and often, during the five weeks that the bad roads kept Steuben waiting for the answers to his letters, his feet trod that long flight of steps and crossed that hospitable threshold which but a few years ago were still standing to tell of the olden time and Boston's provincial splendor. At last Washington's answer came, courteous though formal, and referring him to Congress as the only body authorized to accept offers of service or make appointments. At the same time Hancock informed him that he had been directed by Congress to make every preparation for securing him and his suite a comfortable journey to York, in Pennsylvania, where Congress was then sitting. Hancock was not the man to do this work negligently. The ground was covered with snow, and sleighs with five negroes for drivers and grooms were prepared for the baggage, and saddle-horses for the general and his suite. A purveyor, too, accompanied them to provide provisions and quarters. The enemy were in possession of Newport and New York, and made frequent incursions into the interior. A roundabout course, extending to four hundred and ten miles, was the only course Steuben and his party could take without exposing themselves to unnecessary danger. The journey began on the 14th of January, and it was the 5th of February before they reached York. Thus at the very outset Steuben gained what to his military eye was an invaluable view of a large section of his new country. He got also a few glimpses of one of its elements of danger, the tory element.

In Worcester County, near the Connecticut border, was a tavern notorious by the ill fame of its tory landlord, and which Steuben had been counseled to avoid. But a snow-storm left him no alternative, and at nightfall his weary train drew reins at the door of evil name. True to his reputation, the landlord told them that if they would stop at his house they would have to take up with bare walls; for he had neither beds, bread, meat, drink, milk, nor eggs for them. Remonstrances and even entreaties were powerless. Steuben's blood began to boil; a copious shower of. German oaths was tried and all in vain. " Bring me my pistols," he cried in German, to his German servant, and while the landlord was looking on with malignant satisfaction he suddenly found a pistol at his breast, " Can you give us beds ? " " Yes," trembled the affrighted miscreant. " Bread ? " " Yes." " Meat, drink, milk, eggs ? " and still " Yes," to each demand. The loyalist saw that the terrible German was in earnest. The table was quickly spread, all wants abundantly supplied, and after a comfortable night and a good breakfast the party resumed their journey, not forgetting to pay the tory liberally in Continental money.

One feature of the journey, however, was very grateful to Steuben's German pride. The Seven Years' War was still a recent event, and Frederick a popular name everywhere, more especially among the Germans. Hence town, village, or wayside inn displayed the well-known sharp features and high shoulders as a sign, and decked its walls with prints in honor of the great king, and sometimes to the disparagement of the "great nation." At Manheim in particular the baron, with a significant glance and great internal enjoyment, called the attention of his French secretary to an engraving on the dining-room wall,

representing a Prussian knocking down a French-
man, with the motto, " Ein Franzmann zum
Preuszen wie eine Mücke " (A Frenchman to a
Prussian is like a gnat).

And now opens the serious chapter of Steuben's
American life. The Congress at York was not
that wise Congress which had declared independence and launched the new " ship of state " upon
its perilous voyage, but that weak and divided Congress which had opened its ears to calumnies upon
Washington and almost resolved to set up Gates
as his rival. Gates himself, with a brain whirling
with the excitement of unmerited success, was en-
joying the good dinners and warm quarters at the
temporary seat of government, while Washington
was starving and freezing with his army in the
huts and hovels of Valley Forge. How was Steuben with his five weeks' stock of English to distinguish between the true hero and the false one ?

St. Germain had chosen his man well; an experienced and scientific soldier, for no other could
have done such work as he was appointed to do ;
a man experienced in men, also, and both too wise
and too honorable to become the tool of a faction.
Gates loaded him with civilities and urged him to
stay at his house. But, meeting the civilities
with polite appreciation, he refused the dangerous hospitality.

It became apparent that in counseling Steuben

to assume a rank unknown in the American army, Vergennes, St. Germain, Montbarey, and Miranda had proved themselves wise in their generation. Dazzled by the claim which was so well borne out by his professional knowledge and personal dignity, Congress appointed a special committee to wait upon him and listen to his proposals. They were not such as Congress had been in the habit of receiving; for he told them that he asked for neither rank nor pay, that he wished to enter the army as a volunteer and perform any duty which the commander-in-chief might assign him, and that commissions for his aids and the payment of his actual expenses were the only conditions which he should stipulate, leaving the question of ultimate compensation to be decided by the success or failure of the struggle. No time was lost in idle discussions. The committee reported without delay. The next day he received a formal entertainment from Congress as a mark of special honor; members and guests gazing upon him, as in his rich uniform and with the star of his order which never left his breast he sat at the right hand of President Laurens, and arguing well for the army which was to be trained by a man of such a keen eye and soldierly bearing. Then when the dinner was over, the president handed him the resolutions of Congress.

" *Whereas*, Baron Steuben, a lieutenant-gen-

eral in foreign service, has in a most disinterested
and heroic manner offered his services to these
States as a volunteer,

" *Resolved*, That the president present the
thanks of Congress, in behalf of these United
States, to Baron Steuben, for the zeal he has
shown for the cause of America and the disinterested tender he has been pleased to make of his
military talents, and inform him that Congress
cheerfully accepts of his services as a volunteer in
the army of these States, and wish him to repair
to General Washington's quarters as soon as con-
venient."

Steuben lost no time in setting out for camp.
The ovations continued. At Lancaster the German population felt all their national pride revived at the approach of such a German. A sub-
scription ball was given in honor of his arrival,
and great was the mutual satisfaction as they
looked upon his noble bearing and brilliant deco-
rations, and he heard once more from woman's
lips the accents of his native tongue. While he
was yet some miles from camp, Washington came
out to meet him and conduct him to his quarters.
There a guard of twenty-five men had been stationed, with an officer at their head. Steuben
would have declined the honor, saying that he
was merely a volunteer. "The whole army,"
said Washington, "would gladly stand sentinel

for such volunteers." The next day the troops were mustered, and Washington accompanied Steuben to pass them in review.

During part of his life, at least, Washington was a soldier at heart. When he first heard the bullets whistle he found " something charming in the sound." [1] He had often said that " the most beautiful spectacle he had ever beheld was the display of the British troops " on the morning of Braddock's defeat.[2] And even after he had declared that " he scarcely could conceive the cause that would induce him to draw his sword again," [3] he wrote to Lafayette that " as an unobserved spectator he would be glad to peep at the Prussian and Austrian troops at their manœuvrings on a grand field-day." [4] Thus, when Steuben came to him as a Prussian veteran, he felt that there was a bond between them which they might both cheerfully acknowledge. And, perhaps, he also felt that to bring him at once before the army as the object of uncommon honors was the surest way of preparing it to look up to him as a man capable of imparting to it the knowledge and habits in which it was so universally deficient.

[1] The discovery of a letter of Washington's with these very words in it, confirms Walpole's story, hitherto called in question as inconsistent with Washington's character. Vide Irving, i. 124, note.

[2] Sparks, _Life of Washington_, p. 65.

[3] Lett. to Marquis de la Rouerie, Oct. 7, 1795.

[4] Sparks, _Writings of Washington_, ix. 145.

It was a great relief to Washington's mind to find that he had no longer an unprincipled intriguer like Conway to look to for the reform of discipline, but "a gentleman — a man of military knowledge,"[1] and with that knowledge of the world without which the highest military knowledge would have been of no avail. But it was a serious drawback that he could talk with him only through an interpreter, even though the interpreter was Hamilton or Laurens. At no time in the course of the war had the condition of the army been more distressing. The life at Valley Forge was a daily struggle with cold and hunger; the log and mud huts in which the troops lived were an imperfect protection against the rigor of the winter, made doubly severe by the want of proper clothing and nutritious food. The frequent failure of supplies had familiarized the minds of the men with the idea of mutiny, and brought the officers to feel that if not almost justifiable, it was at least inevitable. There was no assurance of greater regularity or abundance in the future to help bear up against the pressure of the present. Out of the original force of seventeen thousand men, there were three thousand nine hundred and eighty-nine without clothes enough to enable them to mount guard or appear on parade. From desertion and disease, five

---

[1] Sparks, *Writings of Washington*, v. 244.

thousand and twelve men were all that could be called out for duty, and these were so imperfectly armed that muskets, fowling-pieces, and rifles were found in the same company, with a few bayonets scattered here and there ; guns and bayonets alike rusty and unfit for service. These, however, were the men with whom Washington had manœuvred in front and on the flanks of the well-armed and well-disciplined army of Sir William Howe; had fought the battle of the Brandywine, where a portion of them under Greene had marched four miles in forty-nine minutes, seizing and holding a favorable position for covering the retreat of the main body; and the battle of Germantown, where a dense fog and an error of judgment were all that saved the British army from defeat and capture. And they had done all this because they possessed what Burgoyne[1] attributed to the northern army, "the fundamental points of military institution, sobriety, subordination, regularity, and courage. . . . . Their panics were confined and of short duration ; their enthusiasm extensive and permanent." It was to the honor of Steuben's sagacity that, with an eye accustomed to the faultless equipments and precision of movement of Prussian troops, he should have detected those funda-

[1] Letter to Lord G. Germain. Sparks, *Correspondence of the Revolution,* ii. 96, 97, note.

mental points, or the capacity for acquiring them, under the rags and rusty equipments and in the awkward " Indian file " of the American troops. And it was still more to the honor of his energy and force of will that, " without understanding a word of the English language, he should think of bringing men born free, and united for the defense of their freedom, into strict subjection; to teach them to obey without a question the mandates of a master, — and that master once their equal, or possibly beneath them in whatever might become a man." [1]

One of the characteristic acts of the Conway cabal had been the creation for Conway of the office of inspector-general, with powers so extensive as to justify the expression of "*imperium in imperio,*" which Marshall applies to the organization of the commissariat.[2] But, happily for the army, the conspiracy was detected before he had entered fully upon the performance of his duties, and thus one of the immediate results of the attempt to forward the malignant aims of a vile intriguer was to prepare the way for a high-minded and honorable man. In another way, too, the Providence that watched over us had educed good from this evil. Mifflin, the quarter-

[1] *A Biographical Sketch of the Life of Baron Steuben,* etc., by General W. North, Steuben's Aid. Kapp, p. 129, 130.

[2] Marshall's *Washington,* i. 215, 2d ed.

master-general, though originally a member of Washington's family, and intrusted by him with this responsible office " from a thorough persuasion of his integrity," [1] had proved false both to Washington and to his country; neglecting his official duties and entering deeply into the plots of the intriguers. During the hardships of this trying winter he had held himself aloof from camp, and contributed nothing either directly or indirectly to the feeding or clothing of the army. At last a committee was sent by Congress to take counsel with Washington and see what could be done to avert the dangers of " a dissolution, or starvation, or mutiny " [2] which were becoming more and more imminent every day. One of the effects of their exertions and representations was the appointment of General Greene as Mifflin's successor. One of the chief obstacles to the establishment of discipline was thus removed, and if zeal and energy could accomplish it, the army would henceforth be fed and clothed.

Steuben's first step was to draw up a plan of inspectorship, and after revising it with the assistance of Greene, Hamilton, and Laurens, submit it to Washington for approval. Washington approved it, and transmitted it to Congress. There

---

[1] Sparks, *Writings of Washington*, iii. 68.

[2] Nearly Washington's words. Vide, also, for a vivid picture of the state of things at Morristown, Washington to Wayne, Sparks, v. 232, and to Geo. Clinton, v. 238.

was no time to lose. Winter was passing, and the day for opening a new campaign drawing menacingly near. " Will you undertake to execute this plan ? " asked Washington. " With your support and assistance, I will," replied Steuben. He began by drafting from the line a hundred and twenty men, as a guard for the commander-in-chief and a military school for himself. These men he drilled twice a day ; and striking from the outset an effective blow at the prejudice (one of England's legacies) which led officers to regard the drilling of a recruit as a sergeant's and not an officer's business, he took the musket into his own hands and showed them how he wished them to handle it. At every drill his division inspectors were required to be present, and doubtless many officers and soldiers were present, too, without requisition. " In a fortnight," he writes, " my company knew perfectly how to bear arms, had a military air, knew how to march, to form in column, deploy, and execute some little manœuvres with excellent precision."

Hitherto, every attempt to instruct the soldiers had been begun, according to rule, by the manual exercise ; and, now from one cause and now from another, every such attempt had failed. In nothing did Steuben's superiority to a mere martinet appear more decidedly than in his passing the manual by and beginning with manœuvres. The

4

sight of men advancing, retreating, wheeling, deploying, attacking with the bayonet, changing front, and all with promptness and precision. made an impression upon the spectator which no perfection in the mere handling of the musket could have produced. The actors, too, moved by a common impulse, felt that confidence in themselves which men always feel when acting harmoniously together, and learnt, from the outset, to look with double confidence upon the man who had awakened them to a consciousness of their short-comings by "skillfully yielding to circumstances" in the development of their capacities. Every scholar of this school became an apostle of reform. The army that looked on and admired longed to be permitted to share in the lesson. Battalions came next, then brigades, and then divisions. It was on the 24th of March that the elementary manœuvres began, and by the 29th of April, American troops, for the first time since the opening of the war, were able to execute the grand manœuvres of a regular army. On the 5th of May, Steuben was appointed by Congress inspector-general, with the rank and pay of major-general.

·Steuben's success is easily explained. His heart was in his work. He was up before day, smoked a single pipe, swallowed a single cup of coffee, had his hair carefully dressed, his uni-

form carefully put on; and then, as the first
sunbeam appeared, he was in the saddle and off
for the parade-ground. There was no waiting
for loitering aids. No part of his work was beneath him. He took the guns into his own
hands, examined the equipments with his own
experienced eye. Not a voice was to be heard
but his, and that of his officers as they repeated
his orders. Not a mistake passed unreproved.
" Ah," said one of his captains, a captain once,
but then the keeper of a country tavern, " how
glad I am to see you, baron, in my house; but I
used to be dreadfully afraid of you." " How so,
captain ? " " You hallooed and swore and looked
so dreadfully at me once, baron, that I shall
never forget it. When I saw you so strict to the
officers on my right, I felt very queer; and when
you came up to me, baron, I hardly knew what
to do, and I quaked in my shoes." " Oh fie, dear
captain." " It was bad, to be sure, but you did
halloo most tremendously."

The conviction that he was thoroughly master
of what he was teaching them would hardly have
reconciled officers and men to his severity and
" sudden gusts of passion," if they had not been
equally convinced of his justice. Once at a
review near Morristown, Lieutenant Gibbons, a
brave and good officer, was arrested on the spot
and ordered into the rear for a fault which it aft-

erwards appeared another had committed. At a proper moment the commander of the regiment came forward and informed the baron of Mr. Gibbons's innocence, of his worth, and of his acute feelings under this unmerited disgrace. " Desire Lieutenant Gibbons to come to the front, colonel." " Sir," said the baron to the young gentleman, " the fault which was made, by throwing the line into confusion, might, in the presence of an enemy, have been fatal. I arrested you as its supposed author; but I have reason to believe that I was mistaken, and that in this instance you were blameless; I ask your pardon: return to your command. I would not deal unjustly by any, much less by one whose character as an officer is so respectable." [1] All the while he was saying this it was raining violently; and the men who saw him standing there hat in hand before his subaltern, heedless of the rain that poured down upon his unprotected head, never forgot the scene.

Thus far all went on well. Even in their tatters the men began to feel a pride in being soldiers. If some officers were still compelled to mount guard in an old blanket cut into the shape of a dressing-gown, they knew, at least, how to perform the duty of officers on guard. Washington, in general orders, praised their progress and

[1] North in Thacher's *Military Journal*, p. 416.

thanked the man to whom they owed it. But
now arose the question of converting this temporary inspectorship into a permanent inspectorship
with corresponding rank in the line. A reform
in drill was but a small part of the real work to
be done. The whole organization of the army
required reform in all its parts. The quartermaster-general's department was now secure;
the commissariat also. " The internal administration of a regiment and a company was a thing
completely unknown." " The number of men in a
regiment as well as in a company was fixed by
Congress," but some were three months' men,
some six, some nine. There was a constant ebb
and flow, a constant coming and going. Accurate returns of such regiments were out of the
question. " Sometimes a regiment was stronger
than a brigade;" sometimes it contained but thirty
men, and a company but a single corporal. The
men " were scattered about everywhere." Officers acted as if the army were but a nursery of
servants; each claiming one, many two or three.
And thus many hundred soldiers were converted
into valets. But on the regimental books they
still held their places unchanged; and long after
many of them had ceased to belong to the army
even as valets, pay was still drawn in their
names from the impoverished treasury. Leaves
of absence and even dismissals were given by
colonels and sometimes by captains at will.

While men went and came in this manner, and were thus employed, there could be little hope of preserving the public property intrusted to their hands. Every musket was valued at eighteen dollars with a bayonet, and at sixteen without one. And yet for every campaign from five to eight thousand muskets were required, to replace those lost by negligence or carried off by the men whose terms of enlistment had expired. With the most methodical and systematic of men at their head, it had been utterly impossible to introduce method or system into this ebbing and flowing mass.

Steuben aimed at the correction of all these abuses; but unfortunately, in asking for the powers which he deemed essential for the accomplishment of his task, he asked for some which seemed to trench upon the rights of other officers. Some of the major-generals became alarmed. All the brigadiers, it was apprehended, would resign if his demands were complied with. Whatever Washington's private opinion may have been, he publicly conformed to the public opinion, and issued in June the general orders by which — Congress with its wonted dilatoriness putting off a decision from day to day — the office continued to be regulated till 1779. These orders not only defined the duties but greatly limited the powers of the inspector-general. Steuben saw the cause

and understood it, foresaw, too, the consequences
and deplored them ; but, faithful to his resolution, adapted himself to circumstances, and continued to labor with unabated energy in his daily
drills and special reforms.

Events were already demonstrating the excel-
lence of his work. In May, 1778, Lafayette, upon
the point of seeing himself outnumbered and cut
off from the main body of the army, was able
to save his men by an orderly retreat, in which
their good discipline was manifest. Washington, however, anxious for Lafayette's detachment,
ordered out the whole army to support it ; and
in less than fifteen minutes the whole army was
under arms and ready to march. At Monmouth,
not long after, at the sound of Steuben's now
familiar voice, Lee's broken ranks rallied and
wheeled into line under a heavy fire as calmly
and precisely as if the battle-field had been a
parade-ground.

But the roar of the cannon stirred the old soldier's blood, and he began to feel keen longings
for more exciting work than teaching manœuvres
and examining reports. It so chanced, also, that,
most of the brigadiers being called away by Lee's
court-martial, Washington found it necessary to
give Steuben the temporary command of a division, on the march to the Hudson in July, 1778.
And thus, when directed to resume his duties as

inspector-general, all the vexation and disgust he had felt at the obstacles which had been unnecessarily thrown in his way were renewed, heightened by the refusal of De Neuville, the inspector of Gates's army, to receive orders from him as inspector-general. He now talked freely of his dissatisfaction, objected to the position which he had hitherto worked in so cheerfully, and more than intimated his intention to resign unless his desire for a command in the line were complied with. It was natural, but it was unfortunate, and there can be little doubt but that in a calmer mood he regretted it. Here again Washington's serene wisdom appeared, as it appeared in so many other decisive moments. He did not approve of Steuben's aims, but he appreciated his services at their full value, and continued to treat him with his wonted urbanity, freely acknowledging how much he had done, but carefully abstaining from everything that might have been interpreted into an encouragement of his new pretensions. It was with Congress to decide what the inspectorship was to be and what place the inspector was to hold in the line; and it is not improbable that Washington saw the discontented and more than half angry baron set out for Philadelphia, with confidence that before that dilatory Congress could come to a decision, his natural good sense and love of his profession would prepare him to return willingly, if not cheerfully, to his original position.

For Congress was once more sitting in Philadelphia, in the old hall where the Declaration of Independence had been made. But it was there with a task to perform, to which legislative bodies are altogether unequal: with a responsibility weighing upon it which none but a strong executive could have borne, vainly trying to govern by treasury boards and boards of war, to call out the resources of the country by requisitions and recommendations, and to decide questions which demanded immediate decision as they decided upon laws and acts which demanded careful, full, and deliberate discussion. It was shorn also of some of its brightest ornaments, disturbed by internal dissensions which it no longer had the self-control to conceal, and brought to its discussions a spirit poisoned by jealousy of the army on which it depended for its existence.

It was to this Congress that Steuben brought his claims, and if Washington had counted upon their dilatoriness for giving the baron's anger time to cool or to turn towards a new object, he did not count in vain. One important question was decided at once : De Neuville was made responsible to the inspector-general, thus soothing the German, whose value was felt, and inviting to resignation the Frenchman, whose value was doubted. This made it easier to meet his application for a command in the line, and, appointing a committee to consider the new plans concerning the inspectorship, Congress seemed ready to proceed at once to the discussion of them. But before any decision could be reached, the unfavorable turn which things were taking in Rhode Island afforded an opportunity for postponing the matter indefinitely, and Steuben was requested to go to the assistance of General Sullivan. Thus by the end of August, Sullivan's expedition being ended before he could reach him, although he traveled with the utmost dispatch, he again found himself with the main army. When the army removed to Fredericksburg he was once more actively engaged in the dull routine of manœuvres, drills, and reports.

He seems meanwhile to have become convinced that this was the field in which he could do the most good, and, with the exception of an occasional return of his longing for a more dazzling glory, he resolved henceforth to content himself with the glory of being useful. To induce Congress to place his department upon a permanent footing was henceforth his immediate object; and when the army went into winter quarters he again repaired to Philadelphia. It was an irritating business for a hot-tempered, earnest man, convinced of the correctness of his views, convinced, too, that important as many other things which Congress was busy about might be, there was none in the wide circle of their competency more important than this. All Washington's influence, all the force of Hamilton's representations, were employed in his favor: but still week after week wore away, and February, 1779, was near its end before the question was seriously taken up. Then at last a series of resolutions embodying nearly the substance of his later plans, as revised and approved by Washington, was passed, and, much as they fell short of his original expectations, he was glad to find himself in a position to set himself effectively to work.

But he had not idled away the winter in attendance upon Congress. To make his inspectorship successful it was necessary that every officer should be provided with a uniform system of regulations for the order and discipline of the troops. He had congratulated himself at the outset that no existing work had attained to a sufficient degree of popularity to make it a general standard.[1]

[1] The military bibliography of that period is briefly given by Washington in a letter to a young officer. Bland (the newest edition) stands foremost; also an *Essay on the Art of War: Instructions for Officers*, lately published at Philadelphia. *The Partisan*, Young and others. Sparks, *Writings of Washington*, iii. 154. Among General Greene's books is a *New System of Military Discipline by a General Officer*, published by R. Aitken, printer and book-seller, Philadelphia, 1776, with an appendix containing nine sections of "rules, maxims, etc.," some of

He had found every colonel, almost every captain, with a system of his own, and agreeing only
in marching their men in Indian file. The ground,
therefore, was free, and to fill it aright he composed that volume so long known in the army
of the United States as " Steuben's Regulations,"
or the " Blue Book."   And here again we see his
superiority over mere formalists and drill masters.
With a thorough knowledge of all that had been
done, he knew also what it was possible to do.
Fully aware that in European armies a man who
had been drilled three months was still held to
be nothing more than a recruit, he was equally
aware that in the American army he could not
count upon more than two months for transforming a recruit into a soldier.' Accordingly, taking
less the Prussian system than his own perfect
familiarity with the subject for guide, and with
a wise consideration for the English prejudices
which had struck such deep root in the American
mind, he set himself to his task, with Fleury and
Walker for assistants, De l'Enfant for draughtsman, and Duponceau for secretary. On the 25th
of March the first part was ready for the action
of Congress, having already received the sanc-

the most brilliant of which are " Nothing but principle can conduct a man through life;" " Bad habits are more difficult to
correct than to prevent;" " The mind must be prepared before
it can receive;" " That attack has least effect which is most
obstructed," etc., etc.

tion of Washington and of the board of war. On the 29th, Congress resolved to accept and print it.

Here, again, Steuben's patience was put to a severe test. The printing of his book cost him more oaths than the composing of it. There were but two copper-plate printers in Philadelphia, and one of them so bad that it was found necessary to throw away above six hundred prints. Only one binder was employed, and though a good one, the attractions of privateering were so great that neither he nor the printer could keep men enough together to do half the work they were called upon to do. Steuben was anxious to have two copies richly bound, one for the commander-in-chief, and one for the French minister, but in the whole city there was not gold leaf enough to gild them. His temper failed him more than once, but fortunately the men he had chiefly to do with were Pickering and Peters, who admired and loved him too much to take offense at his sallies. Pickering in one of his letters enters into a full explanation of the causes of delay, and closes with a delicate appeal to Steuben's better feelings: "Should I again discover marks of extreme impatience and even asperity in the inspector-general, I will impute them to his anxiety to introduce a perfect order and discipline in the army, and to his zeal in securing the safety and independence of America." Peters writes with a happy mixture of jest and gravity, promising " to distinguish between the Baron Steuben uninformed, and the Baron Steuben acquainted with facts and difficulties; between the Baron Steuben in good humor and the same gentleman (zoönically) angry and fretted."

At last the work was done; copies were sent to governors of States and distributed through the army, and for the first time since the war began American officers had a clear and definite guide for the performance of their duties.

" Steuben made no delay in putting his theories into practice. He reviewed all the regiments and ordered the introduction of the system of manœuvres contained in the ' Regulations.' " Regiments were formed into battalions, each battalion consisting of a definite number of men. To make sure that the arms and equipments were fit for immediate use, and that the men were not merely men on paper but actually in the ranks, he continued his rigorous monthly inspections. In these inspections there was no trifling, no hurrying over details. Seven hours were not thought too long for the inspection of a brigade of three small regiments. " Every man not present was to be accounted for; if in camp, sick or well, he was produced or visited; every musket handled and searched, cartridge-boxes opened, even

the flints and cartridges counted; knapsacks un-
slung and every article of clothing spread on the
soldier's blanket and tested by his little book,
whether what he had received from the United
States within the year was there; if not, to be
accounted for. Hospitals, stores, laboratories,
every place, every thing was open to inspection
and inspected." The exact, careful man was sure
to be praised and often rewarded; the careless
to be sternly reproved. It took little to move
Steuben's anger; undue delay, misplaced hesitation were sure to do it, and out came a storm of
oaths, German first, then French, and then both
ludicrously mingled; and when the stock was exhausted, turning to his aid, he would say, " My
dear Walker, or my dear Duponceau, come and
swear for me in English; these fellows will not do
what I bid them." A smile would steal silently
over the faces of the men, and the movement be
carefully studied till it was accurately executed.

The crowning labor and complement of all was
the establishment of a system of minute written
reports according to prescribed forms, extending
throughout the whole army and embracing every
department of the service.

In all this work Steuben was but adapting
established principles to the exigencies of a new
case. But in the formation of the light infantry
he became an inventor, sending back a lesson

from the New World to the Old, from Frederick's pupil to Frederick himself. The wars with the Indians had taught Americans to fight, like their adversaries, in loose bodies instead of close masses, each man using his rifle or musket to the best advantage according to his own judgment. These bodies of skirmishers had turned the day against English and German regulars at Bemis's Heights and Stillwater. Steuben organized them into a light infantry with a drill and discipline of their own. Frederick, meditating upon the suggestions of the American war, saw how much such troops might be made to assist the operations of his dense masses, and accepted the improvement. The other armies of Europe followed his example, and from that time they have formed an essential part of every great army and done important service on every great battle-field.

It was soon evident that a new spirit had entered the army. Encampments exhibited the regularity of scientific disposition. Reviews displayed in officers and men familiarity with complex evolutions and that harmony of movement which gives thousands the appearance of a single body under the control of a single will. Inspections demonstrated the possibility of enforcing neatness and exactness and bringing responsibility home to every door. The treasury, which had been repeatedly called upon to pay the services

of men who had long ceased to render service of
any kind, was relieved from a heavy burden by
the introduction of exact rolls and regular reports.
The war office, instead of having to count upon
an annual loss of from five to eight thousand
muskets, could enter upon its record that in one
year of Steuben's inspectorship only three muskets were missing, and they were accounted for.
The opposition and jealousy which had clogged
his first steps, gradually gave way before the
perfect demonstration of his success.   Officers
ceased to shrink from labor with the example of
industry like his before them, or to consider any
part of their duty as beneath them when they
saw him come down from so much greater a
height to do it. " Do you see there, sir, your
colonel instructing that recruit?" he one day
said to North. " I thank God for that, sir."

And no sooner did the soldier find himself in
the presence of the enemy than he showed even
more evidently the change which had taken place
within him.   Hamilton declared that till he saw
the troops forming and manœuvring at Monmouth he had never felt the full value of discipline.   The only use which the few soldiers who
were provided with bayonets had hitherto made
of them, had been as forks to roast their meat
with.   But within less than four months from
the organization of the inspectorship by Con-

5

gress, on the night of the 15th of July, 1779, these same soldiers took Stony Point, at the point of the bayonet and without firing a gun.

Henceforth Steuben's life becomes so mixed up with the general history of the army, or so filled with minute details, that it is impossible to follow it step by step, within limits like ours. It was not all at once that he could carry out his far-reaching views. The army was once more to be remodeled, and he passed weeks at Philadelphia in close communication with Congress and the board of war, keeping up all the time a correspondence with Washington, to whose wishes, from first to last, he was ever ready to conform his own. But Congress again wearied and vexed him by delays, for which the embarrassed condition of the public finances was but a partial justification, and which caused, at times, "the loss of months where it was dangerous to lose days." Private jealousies and personal claims still continued to interfere with the introduction of essential changes. They who have studied the history of this period in the letters of the actors, know that not all our statesmen were wise, not all our officers high-minded, not all our citizens more devoted to their country than to their own pockets. There were times when the whole country seemed heartily sick of the war; and when, perhaps, a Wood or a Seymour, a "New York World" or

an " Evening Express," might have stirred up
thousands to open resistance or lured them on to
treason to their children and their God. For a
time, too, the condition of our finances seemed
hopeless. The currency was worthless ; the public credit gone. The " promise to pay " of the
United States or of the individual States was not
worth the " promise to pay " of a private citizen ; and it was not until the treasury board had
been replaced by a skillful financier that the real
wealth of the country could be brought to the
support of its real interest. In his personal as
well as in his public capacity, Steuben suffered
from these things. But he suffered without losing heart if he sometimes lost patience ; and before the war was brought to a close he had the
satisfaction of seeing himself recognized as the
true organizer of the American army.

Meanwhile he rendered other important services. He accompanied Reed in his survey of the
fortifications of Philadelphia. He took an important part in the movements which preceded the
battle of Monmouth as well as in the battle itself. He rendered valuable service on Washington's staff — the best staff in many respects which
the world had ever seen. He wrote elaborate
opinions and plans of operations which contributed much to Washington's assistance in forming
his own opinions and plans. Some minor services,

too, he performed. He taught the etiquette of receptions and intercourse, when the new French minister visited camp, and trifling as such cares may appear when compared with the grave duties of a general in the midst of such a war, they cease to be trifling when we consider how important it was that the minister's dispatches should represent us as not wholly devoid of a knowledge which the Old World prized so highly. He did service, twice, of a more difficult nature, when he was sent without any ostensible command to supply at West Point the deficiencies of General Howe; and of a more serious nature when, under the presidency of Greene, and with some of the best officers in the army for his colleagues, he sat in judgment upon André. And in all these various duties he demeaned himself so wisely, so tempered and controlled his ardent nature, and manifested throughout such elevation of sentiment and such pure devotion to his adopted country, as to prove that Pickering had interpreted his character well, when in the midst of his perplexities he wrote to him, "Courage, dear baron; those talents which know how to do good without giving umbrage and causing jealousy are always sure to triumph ultimately over all obstacles."

But next to the inspectorship, the field of his most important services was Virginia, in the winter of 1780–81, and during the memorable

and decisive siege of Yorktown. When Greene
was appointed to the command of such fragments
of the southern army as had survived the fatal
day of Camden, Steuben went with him because
there was "an army to be created." With Greene
his relations had been of the friendliest and most
intimate kind, from the day when they sat down
with Hamilton and Laurens, in Steuben's strait-
ened quarters at Valley Forge, to discuss the first
draft of the inspectorship. And now they set out
from Philadelphia together for the field on which
they both felt that the fate of the war was to be
decided, riding the whole of the first day's journey in company; and how pleasantly they jour-
neyed on and how confidentially they talked,
Duponceau in his old age dearly loved to tell; recalling with special satisfaction the evening at
Chester, where Greene, to his astonishment, turned
the conversation upon the Latin poets, and talked
about them like a man who had studied them well.

Greene's chief reliance for men and supplies
was Virginia, and as it was by the organization
of the means of reinforcement and support that
the serious work was to begin, he directed Steuben to take command there and do whatever his
judgment suggested for the accomplishment of it.
And thus the pupil of the Prussian despot was
brought into contact with the American demo-
crat, for Jefferson was then governor of the

State, and governing in a way which has afforded
his adversaries an ample field of crimination, and
cost his eulogistic biographers much labor to defend. The disorder of the finances was great,
but, being an evil common to the whole country,
cannot be accepted as an excuse for the utter
prostration of the government. The departments,
were without a head. The executive acted only
by expedients. The resources were wantonly
wasted by neglect and peculation. The public
arms were scattered; the soldiers and recruits
naked. The militia were so thoroughly demoral-
ized that they plundered with a wantonness that
would have excited wonder in hirelings. A
body of volunteers had been raised at great expense for six months' service. Before they were
all collected the time was so nearly run out that
it was thought better to dismiss them at once
than to send them to the support of the southern
army. Other corps were raised with the same
shortsightedness, and dismissed to save the expense of feeding them. How far a vigorous executive might have prevented these abuses and
errors, and how far it became a party to them by
retaining a hopeless position, we shall not now
pause to inquire.

That in this situation Steuben should have
often lost his temper is easily conceived; that
he should sometimes have strained his authority

to the utmost was perfectly natural. His military eye saw that the fate of Virginia was bound up with that of the Carolinas, and that the surest way to defend her was to strengthen Greene's army. The militia that refused to follow the southern commander beyond Ramsay's Mills, because, unless they set out for home immediately, the time they were called out for would expire before they could reach it, might have enabled him to overtake the retreating and disheartened enemy, follow up the blow which had almost shattered Cornwallis at Guilford, and avert the invasion which cost Virginia some blood and much treasure. In spite of obstacles Steuben persisted in his labors. It was by his energy and judgment that Arnold's invasion was so far checked that the traitor was able to accomplish but a part of the evil he had meditated. It was to him, also, that part of Lafayette's success was owing; the old general having prepared the way which the young general followed so happily. But still, of all his hard experience of life, this was the hardest; and it was with an indescribable feeling of relief that he found himself in the lines before Yorktown.

His first siege had been the siege of Prague, as a volunteer, when a boy of fourteen; his last the siege of Schweidnitz, as Frederick's aid, at the close of the Seven Years' War. And now, in the trenches at Yorktown, he saw another great war drawing rapidly to its end, and bringing with it the end of his own long and honorable military career. He was the only American officer who had ever been present at a siege, and here, as on so many occasions, his experience was of great service. It was the only time, too, that he had ever had the command of a division, and fortune so far smiled upon him as to bring on the first overtures for surrender during his term of duty in the trenches; thus giving him the privilege, so highly prized by soldiers, of being in actual command when the enemy's flag came down.

When the victorious army returned northward he returned with it, to resume his place as inspector-general; a minute, laborious, and for most men a wearisome round of monotonous duties, but which, under the influence of the spirit which he brought to it, was now universally recognized as the indispensable basis of good military organization. Never was the discipline of the troops more perfect than during the last two years of the war; and it is surely not claiming too much for Steuben to say that the sense of duty and subordination which that discipline cultivated was not the least among the causes which enabled an impotent Congress peacefully to disband an injured and irritated army. Authentic anecdotes have been preserved of the pride which he took in showing off to the best advantage the acquisitions of his military children, and of the confidence with which they came to look up to him as a father. One of the reviews at Verplanck's Point was roughly sketched by North. If we imagine Washington's marquee on an eminence, with the richly wooded scenery of the North River for a background; Washington himself standing before it, surrounded by French and American officers; in the foreground Steuben, on horseback, with a glow of triumph in his hazel eye as he watches with proud bearing the evolutions which it was supposed none but a Prussian army could execute, and the Hudson girding in the scene and partly reflecting it in its dark waters, we shall have a noble subject for a painter.

Steuben's last public service during the war was a journey to Canada to make arrangements for taking possession of the military posts which were to be ceded to us at the signing of the peace; a service for which his familiarity with the laws and usages of war peculiarly fitted him. Another service which he rendered was in the formation of plans for a military academy; and we commend to the attention of those whose duty it is to watch over our great institution at West Point a careful meditation of that part of his project in which he provides for full professorships of history and geography, of civil and in-

ternational law, and of eloquence and belles-let-
tres. It was probably from him, too, that the
first suggestion of the " Cincinnati " came, and,
had his counsels been followed, the disbanding of
the army, instead of being done stealthily, like
something that Congress was afraid to do, would
have been done in the broad daylight with the
solemnity with which a great people performs a
great duty.

And now, the war being at an end, he would
gladly have gone back to Europe to enjoy his
glory and talk over his American life with his old
friends. But in coming to America he had transferred his benefice of Havelsberg to a nephew,
and exhausted all his other resources; freely ex-
changing the independence which he had won by
long service for the chances of success in the new
cause to which he devoted himself. Unfortunately,
however, instead of following Vergennes' advice
and Lee's example, and making a definite contract with Congress, he had contented himself
with their unrecorded acquiescence in his offer
to make his compensation depend upon the success of the war. And thus, when the war had
succeeded and he asked for a settlement of his
claims, Congress asked for the proof of his contract; and although unquestionable proof of the
nature of his original agreement with the Congress committee was given by the members of

that committee, although the importance of his services was established by the testimony of the whole army, although Hamilton supported his claims in Congress and out of Congress, and Washington went in his favor to the utmost extent which the limits he had prescribed to himself in his relations with Congress permitted, it was not till after an eight years' struggle with poverty that Steuben obtained a final settlement. Then, indeed, his claims were partly, if not fully acknowledged, and an annuity of twenty-five hundred dollars settled upon him. How he suffered meanwhile, he, the large-hearted, free-handed, high-spirited man, from personal privations and public insult; how he suffered, not merely from the actual want of the day, but from the ever present menace of the morrow, and, keenest pang of all for a heart like his, from the inability to relieve the sufferings of others, is a story which fortunately our limits do not permit us to repeat. We commend it to the serious attention of our readers in the clear, minute, and incontrovertible narrative of Mr. Kapp.

During this interval most of his time was passed in New York, where his extensive information, refined manners, and genial sympathies made him a general favorite. Disqualified by his age from entering upon a new profession, he could not settle contentedly down in idleness, or see the new republic, which he had helped build up, silently drifting into anarchy and bankruptcy, without a strong desire to see what lessons might be drawn from history for his instruction. His papers bear witness to the interest which he took in the political occurrences and questions of the day, as well as to the extent of his reading and his habit of patient thought. Like most of those who had been brought into close relations with the Congress of the confederation, he was the advocate of a strong and effective central government, and, had he lived, would have witnessed the overthrow of the federalists with as keen regret as Hamilton himself. Among his studies of this period is a plan for a peace establishment of the army which Washington approved, and a few years later he proposed a plan of fortifications for New York which became the basis of the plan adopted upon the approach of our second war with England. At one moment, despairing of obtaining a settlement with Congress, he turned his thoughts westward and drew up a plan for the establishment, with the sanction of the Spanish government, of a colony in the Spanish territories on the Mississippi. But Spain wanted no such colonists, and his memorial remained unanswered. In 1797 he was chosen one of the regents of the University of New York; a tribute of respect which must have been singularly gratifying to his feelings. A more important expression was given by New York, Virginia, Pennsylvania, and New Jersey, to their sense of his services by large grants of land, and could he but have got money enough to have made these grants available he would have been an independent man.

At length, as we have said, his claims upon the nation were acknowledged. Henceforth he had a fixed income, knew what he could afford to undertake and how he could afford to live. To take up and settle his lands would supply a pleasant occupation for his declining years. Wherever an old soldier was to be found he was sure to find a friend, and as disappointment had neither hardened nor embittered his heart, it was to friendship that he looked for "happiness." It was too late to think of returning to Europe, even if his pecuniary embarrassments had permitted it. America was now his home. And thus, with such hopes as childless old age may indulge in, and such aspirations as had survived thirteen years of active participation in great events and a ten years' experience of court, he entered upon the last phase of his career.

The sixteen thousand acres of land which New York had given him lay in Oneida County, about twelve miles north of old Fort Schuyler, the Utica of our day, and formed part of the township which still bears his name. It was a rough, stony tract, fitter for grazing than planting, with a high ridge running across it, from which, as his eye became familiar with the landscape, he could distinguish the highlands of seven different counties, and, gleaming over the tree-tops on the farthest verge of the horizon, the bright waters of Oneida Lake. This was to be his home during the active months of the year, and when the cold months came and armies went into winter quarters, he would turn 'his face southward and resume his station at 216 Broadway, opposite St. Paul's Church. As a landholder he could indulge his generous impulses, and more than one who had no other claim upon him than what the name of old soldier gave, received a grant of sixty or a hundred acres, either as a free gift or on terms that differed little from it. As a farmer he could indulge his old habits of methodic organization and a methodic division of his time. Sixty acres were set apart and cleared for the manor-house, which was to be a building suited to his rank and habits of life. Meanwhile he contented himself with a log-house, enlarged after a short time by the addition of a frame-house of two rooms. Here Mulligan, then a young man fresh from Columbia College, and who served him as secretary, was his constant inmate; North, or Walker, or some other old companion, would often come to stay a week or more with him, and some of his nearer neighbors, the most welcome among whom was a Dutch emigrant named Mappa, a gentleman of distinguished ability and high culture, loved to visit him and talk over the questions of the day and the news from Europe. This news he got from the " Leyden Gazette," the " Galignani's Messenger " of those days, and inexplicably strange it seemed to him, at times, especially when he read therein that the Prussian eagles had turned back in ignominious retreat before the tricolored flag of the new republic.

He studied farming as he had studied the art of war, by method and rule, entering everything in his diary and recording his progress step by step. The minute accuracy of the inspector-general pervaded the daily habits of the farmer in his clearing. And never, perhaps, even as he rode his war-horse down the line, looking, as one who saw him describes him, " like the god of war himself," did he feel a truer pleasure than when he guided Molly, his quiet little mare, through the stumpy and half-worn paths of Steuben. In the evening chess or a book filled up the time pleasantly, Voltaire being one of his chief favorites, and Gibbon, whose great history had soon found its way across the Atlantic, coming in for a share of his attention. Of German literature, although it had already entered upon the brightest period of its marvelous development and might have held out, at least in the "Revolt of the Netherlands" and the "Thirty Years' War," great attractions for one who had himself been an actor in a great revolt and a great war, his biographer makes no mention, leaving us thereby to conclude that, like Frederick, he had failed to comprehend this part of the great changes that were going on around him. And thus the last four years of his life glided smoothly away, with little in them to recall Frederick's camp, or the drawing-rooms at Hechingen, but with something of a grateful variety, and much to awaken a placid interest. Loving much and much beloved, he had reached unconsciously, but not unprepared, the brink of the grave.

His last appearance in public was as president of the German Society, in New York, when with drums beating and banners displayed he marched at their head from the Lutheran school-house in Nassau Street, down Broadway and through Whitehall, to see them do their voluntary day's work upon the fortifications of Governor's Island. His last service to the country was in the summer of 1794, as president of the board of commissioners for fortifying the northern and western frontiers of the State; a work which filled up the whole summer, and was very near ending in capture by the Indians.

The winter of 1794 began early. In November the ground was already covered with snow. The log-hut began to look sad and lonely in the cold, white landscape. Little Molly could no longer make her way through the clearing. North's visit was over. Mulligan was alone with him, with the two servants. The regular time for going to New York was not quite come, but he resolved to anticipate it, and made all his preparations for the journey. The 25th of November came. There was no change in his firm tread, or the clear ring of his voice, or the kindly light of his hazel eye. He played his game of chess, he listened while Mulligan read; at eleven, his usual bedtime, they parted for the night. He had been for some years a communicant of the Lutheran Church, and before he laid his head upon his pillow, we may well believe that he had bowed it in prayer. Then came a few hours of sleep, and in sleep the death-stroke, sudden but not instantaneous, and made bitter by great agony. His servant ran to call Mulligan. "Do not be alarmed, my son," Steuben said, as he saw his young friend rush into the room in terror. The motion of the left side was gone. He asked to be taken up, but returned quickly to bed again. The agony continued. By six he was speechless. It was not till the afternoon of the next day that a physician could be procured. He was still breathing and, for a while, sensible. Remedies were applied, and with a momentary gleam of hope. Then he became unconscious, though breathing still. The night wore away, with occasional returns of convulsions but none of consciousness. The vigorous frame which had borne up so stoutly against cold and hunger, against sleepless nights and days of toil, struggled painfully with death. The faint breathing alone told the weeping attendants that he was yet alive. Towards noon it grew fainter and fainter, and at half past twelve of the second day it ceased.

North had been sent for, but the roads were so bad that all was over before he arrived. Mulligan had made most of the preparations for the funeral, and as the two mourners talked them over, they remembered that their friend had once pointed out a hemlock-tree on the north of the house as a good place to be buried in. There, then, they had a grave dug, although the snow around it melted and made it hard to keep it clear; and thither on the next day about noon, the neighbors, some thirty in all, joining with them, they bore him in silence and laid him down to his rest.

Alas that for this wearied and war-worn frame it should not have been the last rest! But early in the present century the town, which had outgrown the memory of its highest honor, wanted a road, and the engineer who laid it out ran it over Steuben's grave. The coffin was laid bare, remaining exposed for some days to idle gazers and the chances of the weather. It is even said, and we fear with too much truth, that some one, a little more daring in sacrilege, broke it open and tore off a piece of the military cloak. At last the shameful story reached the ears of Colonel Walker, who, hastening to the spot, had the coffin taken up and removed to a neighboring hill-side, where, under the shade of primeval trees, with fragrant flowers laughing all around, and within sound of a little brook whose waters chime sweetly with the music of the winds and the birds, a simple slab still bears the name of Steuben.

And now, if we undertake to assign him his rank in general history, although we should hesitate to call him a great man, we should feel fully justified in assigning him a prominent place among eminent men. In all the situations wherein he was placed he rose above the common level, and that he rose no higher must be attributed to the force of circumstances rather than to any want on his part of the power to rise. To have risen during the Seven Years' War from a lieutenant of infantry to a responsible office on Frederick's own staff was a surer mark of superiority than the command of a division in any other army of those days. To have adapted the improvements of

Prussian discipline to an army of freemen fighting
for freedom required a fertility of resources, a
familiarity with general principles, and a knowledge of human nature, which none but minds of a
high order possess. To have done well whatever
he undertook to do justifies the assumption that
if circumstances had permitted him to undertake
more he would still have done it well. Yet his
methods were rather those of laborious industry
than of that pervading power which constitutes
greatness, or those rapid intuitions which consti-
tute genius. He studied, thought, elaborated his
thoughts, and translated them into action. But
the paths that he marked out could all be distinctly traced to a well-known starting-point ; and
while you follow him with implicit confidence,
you feel nothing in your confidence of that enthusiasm which was inspired by Napoleon, or that
awe which was inspired by Washington. You
would trust, obey, admire him ; but there would
be no absolute renunciation of self in your trust,
no enchaining of will in your obedience, no overwhelming wonder in your admiration. Men
looked up to him, and justly ; but not as they look
up to those heights which rise immeasurably beyond the reach of industry and force of will. For
industry and force of will he possessed in a remarkable degree, combined with clearness of conception, steadiness of purpose, and accuracy of

thought. His mind was eminently sound, his heart warm, and all through a life of camps and courts, overflowing with sympathy and benevolence. His culture was drawn mainly from French sources, but largely modified by strong German instincts, and the habits of German life. A few years later and he would have been a German patriot; and it was happy for him that, born in the age of cosmopolitan civilization, when the soldier of fortune was free to choose his banner and held to fight faithfully for it only as long as he remained under it, circumstances should have led him, after having won his training in the service of a great king, to apply it faithfully and honorably to the defense of a new republic. .

In the military history of our Revolution, if we class men according to their services, no one after Washington and Greene stands so high as Steuben. For the services which Lafayette rendered, important as they were, were rather the effects of influence and position than of individual superiority. All that Steuben owed to position was the opportunity of action; the action itself was the fruit of his own strong will and thorough knowledge of his science. He was the creator of our regular army, the organizer of our military economy. The impress which he made upon our military character remained there long after his hand was withdrawn. The system of drills and manœuvres which in 1779 he drew up in German, to pass through bad French into English, continued to be the system by which all our regulars and militia were formed, until new modifications had been introduced into the art of war by the great wars of the French Revolution. Upon this point the testimony of Washington, Greene, Knox, Hamilton, Pickering, Peters, is uniform and decisive. He claimed nothing to which his claim is not fully borne out by what they wrote and said. His system of reviews, reports, and inspection gave efficiency to the soldier, confidence to the commander, and saved the treasury not less than six hundred thousand dollars.

The private life of a man so large a portion of whose life was passed in the performance of public duties affords little room for the growth of distinctive characteristics. There was a slight haughtiness in his manner which would appear to have been the reflection of his military habit of command rather than the product of arrogance or unbecoming pride; a manner which seemed to say, I know my own position and worth, and expect you to recognize them; but I am equally ready to acknowledge yours. His pride never seems to have degenerated into vanity, that unbecoming mantle in which so many great men have more than half enveloped their greatness, but was a soldierly pride throughout, founded upon the consciousness of what he had done and was still able to do. In society he always appeared to advantage, particularly in that test of true refinement, the society of ladies ; and if his bow savored somewhat of formality, his vein of compliment and humor was always happy. "Ah, madam," said he, bowing low, on being presented to a beautiful Miss Sheaf, and studiously mispronouncing the name, "I have always been cautioned to avoid mis*chief*, but I never knew till to-day how dangerous she was."

Of his generosity innumerable anecdotes have been preserved. Like Goldsmith, he could not withhold even the last penny in his purse when want or suffering asked for it. How often he shared it with the destitute, how bitterly he felt the ungenerous conduct of Congress which made it impossible for him to give as freely as his heart would have dictated, how munificently he employed his opportunities as a land-holder to provide some old soldier with a home, are things which his contemporaries well knew and which posterity should not forget.

GENERAL JOHN KALB.

Verga gentil di picciola gramigna.
The noble scion of ignoble seed.

DANTE, Purgatorio, xiv.

GENERAL JOHN KALB.[1]

On the 29th of June, 1721, John Kalb, the
child of Hans Kalb and Margaret, his wife, peasants, was born in the German town of Hütten-
dorf. On the 19th of August, 1780, Major-
General Baron de Kalb died prisoner of war in
the American town of Camden, of wounds received three days before, in the defeat of the
American General Gates by the English General
Cornwallis. How and when did this peasant
become a baron, and mingle his name with great
historic names and great historic events? We
find him at school at Kriegenbronn, a peasant
boy still. We see him leave his native place
at sixteen to earn his living as a butler. We
lose sight of him for six years, and suddenly

---

[1] *Leben des Amerikanischen Generals Johann Kalb.* Von
Friedrich Kapp, mit Kalb's Portrait. "In deiner Brust sind
deines Schicksals Sterne." — Schiller. Stuttgart: Cotta' scher
Verlag. 1862.

. *The Life of John Kalb, Major-General in the Revolutionary
Army.* By Friedrich Kapp. New York: privately printed.
MDCCCLXX.

find ourselves face to face with him again towards the end of 1743, with the distinctive *de* between the Jean and Kalb of his half gallicized name, and the rank of lieutenant in the regiment of Löwenthal, a body of German infantry in the service of France. Had his regiment been composed of Frenchmen, it would have been easier to conceive how this young Ariovistus, six feet high, with his searching brown eyes, his ample forehead that suggested thought, his distinctly chiseled nose which like the great Condé's suggested the beak of the eagle, the self-control and quiet consciousness of strength which mingled upon his lips somewhat as they did on Franklin's, and the aristocratic double chin and haughty mien, could have passed himself as a noble in times when the herald's office was consulted less than the air and bearing of the claimant of a title. But it was composed of Germans, familiar with the name and grades of German nobility and rigorous advocates of its privileges. By what arts or by what chance did our young adventurer succeed in persuading them that he was a nobleman? How, too, did he, in six short years, succeed in transforming the obsequious butler into the proud baron? That he did thus pass from a peasant to a noble, and put on, as though they had been his birthright, the air and bearing of nobility, is a fact which Mr. Kapp has fully es-

tablished, although he has not been able to explain it, 'and, accepting it as one of the secrets
of history, we pass directly with him from the
peasant's cottage to the camp in Flanders.

Frederick of Prussia, the greatest general of his
own day, was the teacher of Steuben, the subject of Mr. Kapp's first contribution to American
history. Kalb's teacher was Marshal Saxe, "the
professor," according to Frederick himself, "of all
the European generals of his age." And thus
the lessons of the two greatest soldiers of their
time passed through two brilliant adventurers to
the camp of Washington. Both lives belong in
part to the American historian. Toward the
end of 1743, when Washington was going to Mr.
Williams's school at Brydges Creek, and Greene
was a babe in the arms, Kalb comes into the light
of history as a lieutenant in one of the most brilliant German regiments in the service of France.
In a single year he took part in three sieges and
one hotly contested battle ; and still following
the history of his regiment, through which only
we can trace his own, we find him at Fontenoy
and every decisive action of the war except the
battles of Lafeld and Raucoup. In 1747 he was
made captain and adjutant, and was intrusted
with the important duties of " officer of detail,"
an office of great responsibility, comprehending
the internal administration of the regiment and

an active correspondence with the minister of war. In his brief intervals of leisure he found time for study, devoting himself chiefly to modern languages and those branches of the higher mathematics which were essential to the scientific departments of his profession.

The eighteenth century, it will be remembered, was still an age of mercenary soldiers. Men of hereditary rank let themselves out for military rank and the chances of military distinction. To be colonel and give your name to a regiment was to open the way to a new ribbon or a new star and the choicest circles. Even the lowest commission was a patent of nobility; for none were entitled to it in the French service who could not trace their claims through four generations. The German regiments in the French service were especially favored, and commissions in them eagerly sought after. "There is not a general officer in Germany," said Prince Ferdinand of Brunswick to Boisgelin, "whatever his nobility, who would not consider himself as very fortunate in being able to enter the service of France. What a happiness to fight by the side of Frenchmen, and live with them in Paris during peace!"

The foreign regiments in the French service were not all upon the same footing. Each had its own contract, and its own articles of war.

Questions of discipline were decided differently in different regiments, one capitulation approving what another condemned. It was the duty of the officer of detail to make himself familiar with all these distinctions, and be prepared to defend the rights of his own regiment before the minister of war ; an office of toil and difficulty, comprising the whole internal administration of the regiment, from the minutest detail to the most difficult question of jurisprudence. The colonel commanded in battle, but the officer of detail conducted the correspondence with the minister of war and the commanding general.

Such were Kalb's duties in the garrisons of Pfalzburgh and Cambrai, during the peace which preceded the Seven Years' War. The records of his regiment bear witness to his intelligence and zeal. But war was approaching. While deciding the European question, the treaty of Aix la Chapelle had left the American question undecided ; and the American question was the question of the age, carrying with it the transformation of dependent colonies into the greatest of republics. War with England was inevitable. Kalb looked to it for honor and fortune. As a first step toward them he addressed a memorial to the minister of marine, containing a detailed plan for the formation of a foreign regiment of marine infantry. Germany, Denmark, Sweden,

England, and above all, Ireland, were to furnish the men, who were to be thoroughly trained to service in different parts of the world, and especially to sudden landings on a foreign coast. An invasion of England has long been a cherished idea of France, and that it is not altogether a vain idea may be argued from the anxiety, amounting almost to terror, with which every repetition of the menace has been received. Kalb aimed high, but he aimed justly. He would have made Irish discontent a source of weakness to England and of strength to France. But he lacked court patronage, and failed.

A minute history of the Seven Years' War would hardly bring the name of Kalb into prominence. He took part in nearly all its great battles, however, and won the favor of De Broglie, the best of the French generals. But his subordinate position kept him in the shade, and his useful devices were counted only as a part of the general history of his regiment. The court intrigue which removed the successful De Broglie in order to make room for the incompetent Soubise, very nearly deprived him of his position. The peace of 1763 found him a lieutenant-colonel in rank, though in fact only a captain by purchase in the regiment of Anhalt. It gave him, however, an opportunity of adding largely to his private fortune, by his successful advocacy of the claims of

several princely and noble families of Wetterau
for supplies furnished the French army during
the war.

The war was over; what was to become of
those for whom war was a profession? Assistant
quartermaster-general, with the rank of lieutenant-colonel, Kalb had strong claims to promotion; but none of his hopes in this direction were
realized. Fortunately the customs of the age
had allowed him to purchase a captaincy in the
Anhalt regiment, for one of whose companies he
had been reported as if in actual command during the last three years of the war. Upon this
he now fell back for the moment, resolved, meanwhile, to push his fortune in another direction.
He had once before tried to make his way by
personal application, and had failed for want of
protection. He was stronger now, by the friendship and protection of men of rank, and for a
while his hopes were high. Eight new staff officers were to be created, and the Marquis de Cas-
tries exerted himself to procure one of the appointments for him. But the new creations were
not made. A vacant lieutenant-colonelcy for which
he had made application was given to another.
It was a severe disappointment. Still, fortune
had not forsaken him.

During the administration of the provident Col-
bert, a Hollander, named Robin, skilled in the

manufacture of cloth, had been allured to France, where his services were rewarded by a patent of nobility. The occupation was handed down from father to son, and at the time of Kalb's visit to Paris, a grandson of the original immigrant was living with his wife upon the fruits of his own and his ancestors' industry, in pleasant retirement at Courbevoye, near Paris. A younger daughter, " accomplished, sprightly, and beautiful," lived with them. How and when Kalb learnt to know them, no record tells; but it is easy to understand how, as he listened to her intelligent and sprightly conversation and looked upon her beautiful face, he thought that with such a being by his side he might forego his commission; and how, as she looked upon his noble form and listened to his tales of siege and encampment and battle-field, she felt that his would be a strong arm to go through life with. She was betrothed to Kalb in the first winter after the peace, and married on the 10th of April, 1764. They were both Protestants, and the marriage service was performed in the Protestant chapel of the Dutch legation.

Kalb was very happy. He had never fallen into the dissolute habits of his times and profession. Temperate in all things but the thirst of glory, he sought happiness at his own fireside. His wife, who had married him because she loved him, felt her love increase as she became more familiar with his sterling qualities of mind and heart. An adventurer hitherto, dependent upon his sword and the protection of the great, he was now the head of an honorable family and the master of an independent fortune. Money, like other gifts of fortune, came flowing in upon him from many sources. He threw up his captain's commission, and retired from service with a pension as lieutenant-colonel.

But he had not read his own heart aright. The memories of his old life, of its adventures, its vicissitudes, its brilliant rewards, began to stir within him. There were higher grades to win, honors and crosses to decorate his breast with, and point him out to the common eye as a man of mark.

Before a year of that domestic life which promised such happiness was over, he was once more knocking at the doors of men in power. His letters to his wife show how warmly he loved her, and how readily she entered into his feelings.

A brilliant opening seemed prepared for him. A celebrated warrior of the school of the great Frederick, Count William of Schaumburg-Lippe, having successfully defended Portugal from a Spanish invasion, had been employed to raise three German regiments for the Portuguese service. Supported by both the De Broglies, Kalb asked for a brigadier's commission in them. He hoped that after a few campaigns in the Portuguese army, he might return to the French army as a general. But the war was not renewed, and the new regiments were not raised.

Thus far Kalb had aimed only at military promotion. A general's commission would have satisfied his highest aspirations ; a cross of St. Louis would have made him happy for the rest of his life. But a new field was opening for him, in which his power of accurate observation and his sound judgment were to be brought into active exercise. It was now that his attention was called for the first time to the dispute between England and her colonies.

French indignation at the ignominious treaty of Paris of 1763, which stripped France of her colonies in North America, had found utterance in the ministry of the Duke of Choiseul. France had reached the lowest depths of humiliation. Her troops had lost their moral strength by a succession of defeats. Her ships of war had been annihilated. Her ships of commerce had been driven from the seas. Even in the Mediterranean, which she had learnt to look upon as her own, they crept stealthily from port to port. Had Pitt remained at the head of the ministry, the house of Bourbon, which he hated so bitterly, would have become a third-class power both in France and in Spain. But the fall of Pitt opened the way, if not for the recovery of all that had been lost, at least for revenge.

Choiseul availed himself skillfully of the opportunity. He resolved to renew the struggle for the mastery of the ocean, and in a few years had sixty-four ships of the line and thirty-six frigates afloat. To make up for the losses in the East Indies and North America, he encouraged the development and commerce of the French Antilles. Santo Domingo, Guadaloupe, and Martinico began to pour their rich harvests into the French markets and extend French commerce into new fields. Already in the first year of his administration he had formed that compact of the Bourbon family which plays so important a part in the history of the times. In the very same year he had begun, through skillful emissaries, to open the way for extending the French power in Corsica and enlarging French commerce in the Levant. Like the great Napoleon nearly half a century later, he resolved to make Egypt his base of operations against the English possessions in the East Indies. The treaty of Paris had been signed in 1763. In 1764 M. de Fontleroy, an agent of the active minister, was sent to North America to study on the spot, and see whether the report that a question of taxation was fast alienating the affections of the British colonists from the mother country was true. In 1766 the answer came. Fontleroy, entering fully into the views of his employer, traveled over the land in its length and breadth, taking careful note of its rich soil, its abundance of grain, its vast stores of iron, its boundless forests of timber, its capacious harbors, and mighty rivers. The inhabitants, he said, were a hardy, bold, and enterprising race, growing daily in wealth and power, and fully conscious of their strength. Choiseul smiled at the flattering report, so favorable to his own wishes, and continued his inquiries. How well they were conducted the extracts from New England sermons still preserved in the French archives attest.

It was evident 'that there was a general fermentation in the colonies, but how extensive, and how like to prove lasting, it was difficult to say. The minister resolved to send a new agent, and fixed upon Kalb for the delicate and difficult office. " M. de Kalb," say his instructions, " will repair to Amsterdam and there direct his particular attention to the rumors in circulation about the English colonies. Should they appear to be well founded, he will immediately make preparations for a journey to America.

" On his arrival he will inquire into the intentions of the inhabitants, and endeavor to ascertain whether they are in want of good engineers and artillery officers, or other individuals, and whether they should be supplied with them.

" He will acquaint himself with the greater

or lesser strength of their purpose to withdraw from the English government.

"He will examine their resources in troops, fortified places, and forts, and will seek to discover their plan of revolt and the leaders who are expected to direct and control it.

"Great reliance is placed in the intelligence and address of M. de Kalb in the pursuit of a mission requiring an uncommon degree of tact and shrewdness, and he is expected to report progress as often as possible."

Honorable as this mission was, it was not without hesitation that Kalb accepted it. "Do not decline the mission with which I have intrusted you," said Choiseul. "I know that it is difficult and requires great sagacity. But I have fixed my choice upon you after much deliberation, and know that you will see no reason to regret it. Ask of me the means which you think necessary for its execution; I will furnish you with them all." It was no longer time to hesitate. On the 2d of May he received his passports, letters, letters of introduction to the French ambassadors at Brussels and the Hague, and twelve hundred francs for his traveling expenses. On the 15th of July he addressed his first dispatch to Choiseul from the Hague.

He had done his duty thoroughly, visiting all the sea-ports of Holland, and conversing with men

who had lived in the colonies. A German who
had passed fifteen years there, and was actually
collecting new colonists to carry back with him,
assured him that, in spite of appearances, the
breach between the colonies and the mother
country was as wide as ever. The English troops
were but twenty thousand in number, and those
twenty thousand were so widely scattered that
they would find it hard to cope with the four
hundred thousand militia of the colonies. The
Germans of Pennsylvania could raise sixty thousand men. The Irish population was numerous
and ready for revolt. The provincial assembly
were resolved to maintain their rights by the
sword. The English, on the contrary, asserted
that the spirit of resistance had been laid by the
repeal of the Stamp Act. Kalb listened attent-
ively to both statements, and suspected exaggeration in both. "This may be said for effect,
and to conceal the actual condition of things,"
was his comment on the English report. "I am
only repeating his assertions, without being convinced of their truth," he says of the German
emigrant. He had early learnt the art of judicious doubt. Choiseul, with his hot Celtic
blood, was more sanguine than his Teutonic
agent.

Meanwhile, the work of raising emigrants for
the colonies went briskly on. At Rotterdam he

saw twelve hundred of them, traveling from Cologne, by way of Maestricht and Herzogenbush. Frederick had forbidden them to pass through his territories. We can form some idea of the discomforts of their passage across the Atlantic from the fact that they were all crowded into four of the small and inconvenient ships of those days. If we would form an idea of the manner in which, at about this same time, Englishmen were lured into emigration, we have only to follow George Primrose in the " Vicar of Wakefield " to the emigrant agent's office in London : " In this office Mr. Crispe kindly offers all his majesty's subjects a generous promise of £30 a year, for which promise all they give in return is their liberty for life, and permission to let him transport them to America as slaves."

Kalb's first dispatch had hardly reached the minister, when tidings of the temporary lull in the tempest which followed the repeal of the Stamp Act reached Europe. He asked for new instructions. " As it is possible and even probable," answered Choiseul, with the sure perception of a true statesman, " that this quiet will not be of long duration, it is the will of his majesty that you should make immediate preparations for a speedy tour to America, in order to satisfy yourself by personal inspection as to the condition of the country, its harbors, ships, land forces, resources, weapons, munitions of war, and provisions — in short, as to the means at our command if disposed, in case of a war with England, to make a diversion in that direction. You will adopt the greatest precautions in sending me your report, and will immediately upon your arrival inform me where to direct such letters as I shall have occasion to write you."

It throws a pleasant light upon Kalb's relations with his wife that he asked the minister to send his " commands and answers " through her. The instructions of Choiseul were promptly obeyed. On reaching London he found that to wait for the monthly packet would· cause a delay of ten days. " I prefer, therefore," he writes, " to take the merchantman Hercules, Captain Hammet, which sets sail from Gravesend to-morrow for Philadelphia." Had he been inclined to superstition he might have looked upon his stormy passage of three months as the forerunner of disaster. On the 12th of January, 1768, he landed at Philadelphia.

An expression in his first report, written three days after his arrival, shows how promptly he had fathomed the real nature of the relations of the mother country to the colonies. He calls them an " invaluable magazine of raw productions, and a most profitable market for English manufactures." Looking at them from this point of view he cannot conceive that the British government will spare any efforts to secure such a mine of wealth. He quickly saw, also, that the dispute was far from being adjusted. In Holland the English party had assured him that the repeal of the Stamp Act had been voluntary. In Philadelphia he learnt that it had been wrung from the ministers by organized resistance. He was struck by the substantial union of the provincial assemblies. He attached great importance to the renunciation by Boston of British commerce. He saw the full significance of the part borne by women in the dispute, a part of sacrifice and self-denial. " They deny themselves tea, they deny themselves foreign sugar. They will have no more fine linens from England, but sedulously ply their spinning-wheels to prepare them linens of their own. Silks, which they cannot yet make for themselves, they will do without." He detects, also, signs of forbearance on the part of the Parliament. The troops treat the colonists with greater forbearance. The commanding general, instead of prosecuting libels and pasquinades, pretends to ignore them; and the authors, though well known, go unpunished. He has not had time to study the military question, but foresees many obstacles to carrying on war with militia, and obstacles equally great to the formation of an army in a country so extensive and so divided.

In one thing he saw that the temper of the colonists had been misjudged. The remoteness of the centre of government inspired them with a spirit of freedom and enterprise ; and their taxes were very light ; but they had no desire to " shake off the English supremacy with the aid of foreign powers." The immediate object of popular hatred was the House of Commons ; of popular admiration, William Pitt.

On the 20th of January he writes again. He has had time to look about him, and to sift and verify his observations. It is very interesting to study the impressions of an intelligent foreigner at this critical moment, and compare them with those of our own public men. America was so little known that the wildest stories were repeated without exciting a doubt ; and it required no common sagacity to form a calm and deliberate opinion in the midst of so many contradictions. A circumstance which caused him no little alarm was to find that his letters had been opened in their passage through the post-office. Would they not all be opened and the information which he had so laboriously collected be read in Downing Street before it reached Versailles ? What, too, would become of his mission if the letters of the minister should be intercepted ? He resolved to forestall the danger by hastening his tour of observation and returning home in April. The

few days that had passed between his first and
second dispatches were sufficient to convince
him that the indignation excited by the Stamp
Act had not been appeased by its repeal. The
declaratory act, by which Parliament claimed the
right to bind the colonies in all cases whatever,
was equally unacceptable, and the tax on tea,
paper, and glass which followed was interpreted
as an indirect method of enforcing the principle
of the Stamp Act. Concerning the nature of this
principle the colonists had no doubt. With taxation went representation. By the English constitution no province could be taxed without being
represented, and "England ought to be content
with the profits it derives from selling the colonists worthless goods at high prices, and purchas-
ing necessaries from them for a song." Neither did
it escape Kalb's attention that an equally bitter
feeling had been awakened by the restraints with
which the Parliament had hampered American
industry. No sooner had the manufacture of iron
become almost equal to that of England than it
was prohibited by law. The same repression of
manufacturing enterprise had been extended to
other branches of industry. Could the colonists
doubt that they were to be systematically cut off
from the most important sources of wealth, and
their prosperity made to depend upon the caprice
of the mother country? And he esteemed the

restrictions imposed upon American commerce
equally unwise and unjust. It was not with raw
material alone that the colonists purchased English goods. The balance of trade was against
them and they were compelled to drain themselves
of their gold and silver to make up the difference.
Now the specie required to meet the demands
of the English merchant was drawn from the
commerce of the colonists with the West Indies
and the Spanish Main ; and as fast as it reached
the hand of the American merchant it passed to
those of the English merchant. But instead of
promoting this commerce, Parliament prohibited
it. Kalb thought that the decrease of specie was
real, but that it was an exaggeration to attribute
it wholly to the decay of the commerce with the
West Indies. " There is reason to suppose," he
writes, " that it is hoarded on account of the disturbed state of affairs. I cannot believe the statements made with regard to the sums exported to
England ; it is pretended that the article of tea
alone has netted them three hundred thousand
pounds. As soon as I can obtain an insight into
this matter I shall report upon it." He looked
to the non-intercourse resolves as a fatal blow to
English industry. " The result of all these facts,"
he writes, " is that the colonies are more than
ever willing to retrench their expenditures and
live exclusively upon their own productions."

On the 25th of January, 1768, he started for New York. It was a long, tedious, and disastrous journey. The land carriage was cold and slow ; the passage of the Delaware was difficult and dangerous. It took three days to reach Princeton. A fresh wind was blowing when he reached the Kill, but it was fair, and the landlord of the Ferry Inn and the ferryman himself said that the passage was safe. There were five men to cross and four horses, and although it was already between eight and nine in the evening they set sail. But no sooner had they reached the middle of the stream than the wind chopped round, and drove the helpless little craft upon a small island half-way between the ferry and the mouth of Fish-Kill Creek, where she sank. The horses were drowned and the baggage lost ; but the passengers, partly by wading and partly by swimming, reached the shore. It was but half a mile from the ferry, but they could not make themselves heard. There was neither tree nor shrub to shelter them from the bleak wind. They huddled close together to get what warmth they might from the contact of their bodies. They stamped with their feet and thrashed with their arms, and walked up and down to keep off the sleep which leads to death. The heavy hours wore slowly on. At eleven the ferry boy died. At three, Mr. George, a passenger. Day came at last, but it was not till nine that they were seen from the shore and a boat sent for them. Benumbed, unconscious, hardly able to move their limbs, they were placed in a sleigh and conveyed to the house of Mr. Mercerau, whose name reappears a few years later in a useful, though not brilliant position in the war of independence. The first instinct of the half-frozen men was to crowd around the fire, and they paid for the imprudence by the loss of fingers or toes, and in one instance, of a leg. The wiser Kalb bathed his feet and legs in ice-water and then ate and went to bed. His baggage was lost, and with it "several hundred louis d'or, the badge of his order, and the key to his cipher." It was not till the end of February that he was able to renew his correspondence with the minister. His time had not been lost, and his report bears the marks of a careful study of his subject.

" The colonies," he writes on the 25th of February, " seem to intrench themselves more and more in their system of opposition and of economy. It is said that the merchants of London are already beginning to feel the effects of this policy ; that in consequence of it the wages of labor are fallen off ; that a number of the trades, by combining among themselves, have destroyed the business of those who worked for less than the established prices." Then passing to the subject of taxation, which he has evidently studied with

great intelligence and care, he embodies his con-
clusions in these words: " The assembly at Boston have just resolved to remonstrate with the
court against the tea tax, as will appear from
the accompanying English documents, which I
inclose in the original in order to excite less suspicion in case this letter should be intercepted.
The dissatisfaction with the impost grows out of
their aversion to being taxed by the Parliament
instead of by the representatives of their own
provinces. It would seem to me that the court of
St. James mistakes its own interest. If the king
would ask the colonies for sums much larger than
the proceeds of the imposts in dispute, they would
be granted without any objection, provided the
colonists were left at liberty to tax themselves,
and, as free subjects, to give their money with
their own consent. During the late war they
have paid enormous sums, larger ones than the
king demanded, because he approached their assemblies with the same formalities as he observed
in calling upon Parliament for subsidies. It is a
matter of surprise that the court has discarded
this advantageous method, and that the people
of Great Britain are ready to subvert the fundamental polity of the kingdom by taxing their fel-
low-citizens without their consent, when they
submit to the same proceeding only at the hands
of their representatives in the House of Commons.

The colonies have the same right; they can only be taxed by their own assemblies. The king would therefore have to make an application for that purpose to every single colony. But the colonies themselves would not favor the last alternative, partly on account of the expense involved, and partly on account of the certainty of finding themselves in a minority on all occasions, which would unavoidably constrain them to participate in every war waged in Europe by England or by the Elector of Hanover. They would prefer a Parliament or a continental assembly, a power which, however, would soon become dangerous to the crown. All classes of people here are imbued with such a spirit of independence and freedom from control that if all the provinces can be united under a common representation an independent state will soon be formed. At all events, it will certainly come forth in time. Whatever may be done in London, this country is growing too powerful to be much longer governed at such a distance. The population is now estimated at three million, and is expected to double itself in less than thirty years. It is not to be. denied that children swarm everywhere like ants. The people are strong and robust, and even the English officers admit that the militia are equal to the line in every respect.

" I have not yet obtained accurate information

as to the number of the militia, but shall soon
be able to submit a reliable report. The English
troops under General Gage, occupying the country from New England to the Gulf of Mexico,
muster sixteen regiments, each of ten companies,
numbering seventy men in time of peace and a
hundred in time of war, besides a company of
artillery and a number of engineers. I believe
I have already mentioned that these troops are
changed every three years." Nor does he hesitate to touch by the wayside upon a kindred question. "From conversations with several prominent individuals here I have learned that the
English government greatly regrets having made
peace with Spain without demanding possession
of the island of Porto Rico, the possession of
which is in every respect so favorable to English
interests. Under the pretext of protecting their
trade, the English government has many men of
war at sea and a large number of troops on the
continent, not to mention those already stationed
on the islands. It is evident that these troops
are so distributed for the special purpose of being
prepared to pounce upon the French and Spanish
settlements on these islands at the first speck of
war. That the English have treated as good
prizes several ships captured near the island of St.
Juan in the course of last year, you have doubtless been informed."

His observations at Boston confirm his observations at Philadelphia and New York. "I meet," he writes, "with the same opinions as in the provinces already visited, only expressed with greater violence and acrimony. The four provinces composing New England — Massachusetts, Connecticut, Rhode Island, and New Hampshire — appear to be more firmly united among themselves, on account of the community of interests, than the remaining colonies. Massachusetts in particular, the most wealthy and populous, gives the impulse and the signal of independence to the rest. In spite of this restive spirit, however, they all, from the leaders down to the humblest citizen, seemed to be imbued with a heartfelt love of the mother country. The inhabitants of this province are almost exclusively Englishmen or of English stock, and the liberties so long enjoyed by them have only swelled the pride and presumption peculiar to that people. All these circumstances go to show but too clearly that there will be no means of inducing them to accept of assistance from abroad. In fact they are so well convinced of the justice of their cause, the clemency of the king, and of their own importance to the mother country, that they have never contemplated the possibility of extreme measures. The government is accused of fomenting the existing discontent for selfish purposes. The inclosed English slip will acquaint you with the internal dissensions on this subject, and reveal the causes of complaint which are urged against the government. I adhere to the opinion that the incendiaries will not alone succumb, but that the colonies will yet have the satisfaction of seeing the mother country admit herself to have been in the wrong, and do her best to repair it."

Nothing struck him with such surprise as the commercial spirit of the colonists. "I am more and more astonished," he writes, "at the number of merchantmen to be seen in the ports, rivers, and bays, from the Potomac and Chesapeake to Boston harbor. And in addition to these, numberless ships are in course of construction. What must have been the trade of these colonies before the disturbances began? Nor am I less struck with the flourishing appearance of the interior. On my return to France I shall report the most minute particulars in this connection."

From Boston, Kalb went to Halifax, making everywhere the same inquiries and obtaining the same answers. The ultimate separation of the colonies from the mother country he looked upon as inevitable, but did not believe that they would ever call in a foreign power to their aid. It was to the steady increase of their population and prosperity, and not to foreign bayonets, that he looked for the final separation.

He had done a great deal of work in a very short time, and developed civil talents of a very high order. His reports contain views of the colonies which threw a clear but sober light upon the aims and character of the colonists and the resources of the country. He saw from the first what our own statesmen were several years in seeing, that the Canadians could not be counted by the French government as allies. " There are," he writes, " but few persons in those immense provinces in sympathy with France. The most devoted to us have left the country since the close of the war, and those who remain are satisfied with their present condition or expect no improvement of it from a change of rulers. Their lands have risen in value, they pay but trifling taxes, enjoy unqualified freedom of conscience as well as all the privileges of the English people, and take part in the management of public affairs. Besides, they have become closely allied with the inhabitants of the neighboring provinces by intermarriages and other ties. I regard it as my duty to speak candidly on all these matters, because I will not deceive you, and do not wish you to be deceived by others. In case of a war with our neighbors beyond the Channel, it would be difficult, therefore, to make a diversion to this part of their possessions. I always recur to my belief that the quarrels of the English with their colonies will terminate to the satisfaction of the latter. A war with us would only hasten their reconciliation, and on the footing of restored privileges, the English court would even direct all the troops, resources, and ships of this part of the world against our islands and the Spanish Main. A foreign war is less hurtful to England than internal discord, which, however, would at once yield to the necessity of defense against a common foe."

To extend the field of his observations, Kalb proposed to go from Halifax to Maine, thence by sleigh to Lake Champlain, and return to New York by the valley of the Hudson. But, meanwhile, a grave difficulty arose. In spite of all the pains he had been at to secure the transmission of his letters, they had reached his wife with the seals broken. It was evident that he was an object of suspicion, and should his communication with the minister be interrupted, it would be impossible for him to continue his work. A task so delicate as that which had been assigned him could not be performed without frequent instructions. He resolved, therefore, to return to France, make new arrangements for his correspondence, and hold himself at the minister's orders if a new mission should be thought necessary. " Even admitting the possibility of a positive rupture," he writes, " the opening of positive hostilities between the court and the colonies cannot but be far distant, as it presupposes the participation of the people, the shipment of large masses of troops, and extensive levies of soldiers and sailors. On the other hand, the colonies, if hard pressed, would make a pretense of submission, to gain time for erecting a navy, concentrating and disciplining their forces, and making other needful preparations."

These reasonings and conjectures of an intelligent foreigner have a deep interest for the student of our revolutionary history. It is evident that Kalb had been strongly impressed with the resources and rapid growth of the colonies. It is equally evident that he detected the foreshadowings and the eventual necessity of independence. Such sources of wealth could not long remain at the unquestioned disposal of a distant central government. A people so enterprising and intelligent and bold could not fail to become independent by their natural growth. Would they begin the struggle now, or, although the quarrel seemed almost forced upon them, would they wait till they were more fully prepared? They had not yet been pushed far enough to make them willing to accept foreign aid. They still loved their mother country, although she did nothing to win their love. What

was the part of France to be in the impending
contest? Evidently that of an interested state,
seeking for an opportunity to avenge itself on an
enemy. And how could that revenge be made
sure? The period of enthusiastic sympathy had
not yet been reached. A premature foreign war
would efface the sense of their wrongs in the
hearts of the colonists and check the crown in its
career of usurpation. Kalb believed that France
would only obtain her end by watching. The
day of separation would surely come. To endeavor to hasten it would be risking all on a single throw when the game was already in her
hands.

There is another value in these reports. They
bear directly on the question of the motives of
France in the treaty of 1778. Of these I have
already spoken in my " Historical View of the
American Revolution." But I would call attention to them again, as Kalb's mission affords the
strongest evidence that whatever may have been
the aims of Vergennes, Choiseul was seeking the
humiliation of England.

In April Kalb sailed for England, and on the
12th of June was in Paris. Of all his reports, five
only had reached the minister. But he had the
materials of other reports in his portfolio, which
he arranged and sent to the duke. Through the
rest of the summer and early fall Choiseul's in-

terest in the colonies was unchanged. But another question had risen which now absorbed his attention. He had long been trying to strengthen France in the Mediterranean by the subjugation of Corsica. And here first comes to view the Garibaldi of the eighteenth century, the Italian Paoli. To seize upon Corsica was to weaken England. Still more deadly was the blow which he meditated through the colonies. By a system common to all, the commerce of each was confined to the mother country. Could this restriction be removed and the productions of North America be admitted into the colonies of France and Spain, what a blow would be given to the commercial prosperity of England! So thought Choiseul. So thought Count Châtelet, the French ambassador at the court of St. James. But the Spanish ambassador, Grimaldi, saw in it the building of the English colonies into a powerful republic, an evil example to the French and Spanish colonies, and his reasoning prevailed. Had he gone a little further he would have foreseen that the colonies were making rapid strides towards independence by virtue of a law more powerful than the decrees of parliaments or kings. Absorbed by these questions the French minister felt that he had no more need of Kalb and his reports, and coolly threw him off. Choiseul was a great minister, but, like most of his class, regarded men as tools, to be taken up and laid down at will. A few months later he found that in spite of all his services, and while his brain was still teeming with designs for the glory of France, he too was but a tool to be cast aside at the caprice of a vile woman and still viler king. Had Choiseul remained in power it is difficult not to believe that the war of independence would have begun under different auspices and led to speedier results. Still, Kalb's mission was not lost, and his reports and the documents which he collected are still classed among the most valuable records of the early efforts of France, after the treaty of Paris, to undermine the power of England in North America.

The next two years were years of deep humiliation for those who loved France. The power of the infamous Du Barry had become absolute. Ministers and officers of every grade were dependent upon her favor. The king himself was seen standing hat in hand by her carriage at a public review. The downward impulse which society had received from the licentious administration of the Duke of Orleans reached the lowest point of degradation during the last years of Louis XV. The position which the bold bearing and broad statesmanship of Choiseul had won for France was lost by the incompetence and corruption of his successor. A bold and resolute inter-

vention might have prevented the partition of
Poland. D'Aiguillon could only negotiate and
intrigue ; and it should not be forgotten that
England was compelled by the menacing character of her relations with her colonies to confine
her action to an unheeded protest. Individual
sympathy found a stronger expression, and French
and English officers, acting upon their own responsibility, were found in the Polish army.
Kalb was urged to join them, but upon terms
that he could not accept. It was not till Vergennes was firmly seated in the chair of foreign
affairs that America was again a subject of interest in the French cabinet.

For Kalb these years were not without their
pleasures, although tranquil beyond any others
of his restless life. They were years of domestic
happiness and that pleasant provision for the future which so naturally follows the appearance of
children at the fireside. He bought the château
of Milon la Chapelle with its lands and feudal
rights. He made a general arrangement of his
affairs ; and, carrying into private life all the
order and method of his public life, won for himself that independence which accompanies freedom from pecuniary cares. Still the ambitious
and active nature would out. No chance of promotion escaped his watchful eye. He was only
a colonel ; he longed to be a brigadier. He had

done meritorious service. He could not be happy without a ribbon or a cross to tell it by. Nature had given him a vigorous frame and great powers of endurance. Tranquil walks over his own grounds, though accompanied with the feeling that they were his own, that every tree that he planted, every path that he opened, would add to their value for himself and his children, could not satisfy his longing for excitement and motion. The duties and resources of domestic life were insufficient to satisfy the demands of his active and aspiring nature. But while Louis XV. lived, all his efforts to obtain active service failed. The accession of Louis XVI. opened brighter prospects. His friends and early patrons, the two brothers De Broglie, returned to court, and soon we find Kalb in active life. A new rule of service required that retired staff officers should from time to time do duty in garrison, and when in 1775 the Count de Broglie went to Metz as military commander-in-chief, he took Kalb with him. His exemplary performance of his duties won him a warm recommendation to the Count of St. Germain, the new minister of war. " When you shall have returned here, M. le Comte," wrote the minister, " we shall see what disposition may be made of M. de Kalb." America, too, was looming up on the political horizon again, and Vergennes, like Choiseul, hated England. Kalb's hopes were now high. The minister of war gave him a private audience, and he obtained a furlough of two years. He asked for a brigadiership, but there was no vacancy, and the grade of maréchal de camp was promised him instead. In November the question of promotion was decided by a commission of brigadier-general for the islands. It was in the colonies that he was to win his grade. This period of his career deserves a careful study for its connection with the history of the French alliance. It was a period of secret negotiations and public disavowals, of promises made or broken according to the exigencies of the hour, of half-concealed distrust and secret preparation. Never was diplomacy more stained with deceit. Lord Stormont had spies on the track of Vergennes. The spies of Vergennes kept close on the traces of Lord Stormont. France and Spain were in sincere accord with regard to England. But the full story of the wiles and craft by which the way was prepared for the treaty of 1778 would carry us too far beyond the circle of Kalb's individual action. We confine ourselves to that, and find enough there to afford important side lights for the general picture.

Kalb now knew what was expected of him by the government, and what he might expect from

it in return. Assistance was to be given to the
colonies as far as it could be done without com-
promising France. War was to be avoided as
long as possible, and accepted only when the
Americans had given unequivocal proofs of their
strength and perseverance. With this view arms
and money were to be supplied secretly, and for
this purpose Colonel du Coudray, an artillery
officer of distinction, was sent on an apparent tour
of inspection to the forts and arsenals, but with
secret instructions to select an ample supply of
arms for the use of the insurgents. It is in this
connection that we first meet the name of Beaumarchais in American history. Kalb was to go
as a volunteer, on leave, and without imperil-
ing his position in the French army. Too cautious to hazard himself without a positive agreement with some trustworthy agent, he resolved
to wait the arrival of Silas Deane, the secret
agent of the Americans, who was daily expected
at Paris. Of this somewhat equivocal character
in American history I have already told as much
as the occasion required in the work referred to
above. He eagerly grasped at the opportunity of
securing the services of so experienced an officer,
and assured him of the grade of major-general,
with rank from the 7th of November, 1776. Kalb
and Vergennes would have smiled could they
have seen the closing sentence of the dispatch in

which the unskilled agent announced the negotiation to Congress. " This gentleman," he
writes, " has an independent fortune, and a certain prospect of advancement here, but being a
zealous friend to liberty, civil and religious, he
is actuated by the most independent and generous
principles in the offer he makes of his services to
the States of America." On the 1st of December
a formal contract was signed, Kalb affixing his
name to it for himself and fifteen others. On
the 7th of December a new contract was signed,
and on this we find the name of Lafayette, the
first time that we meet this beloved name in
American history. This important transaction
did not escape the watchful eye of the English
ambassador, who immediately reported it to his
government. But England did not want a war
with France, and delayed her revenge.

Meanwhile the arms and military stores destined for the insurgents reached different ports at
which they were to be embarked ; a large number
of officers also appeared in the streets of Havre
and other seaport towns. Love of adventure,
thirst for distinction, an ill-defined zeal for the
rights of men, had kindled the enthusiasm of the
young nobility. Some of them, of large fortunes
and high rank, resolved to take an active part in
the contest. But instead of following the course
which the relations between France and England

required, they talked loud in the streets, discussed their plans in coffee-houses, and went further than Lord Stormont's spies in supplying him with materials for remonstrance. Even the shrewd Beaumarchais, forgetting his *rôle*, gave the rein to his vanity as a dramatist, and had some of his plays brought out on the stage at Havre.

On the 14th of December the Amphitrite sailed with Du Coudray and his suite. Like Kalb, Du Coudray, on reaching Philadelphia, was to rank as major-general, thus outranking native officers of the highest merit. When the tidings reached the colonies it excited a menacing dissatisfaction. But for the moment the danger was averted. The accommodations of the Amphitrite and the storage of her cargo were found unsuitable for a long voyage, and she returned to L'Orient. With such evidence in his hands. Lord Stormont addressed an energetic remonstrance to the French minister, who, not yet prepared for war, forbade the expedition. At this critical moment arrived the tidings of the disheartening campaign of 1776. Vergennes felt that the hour was not yet come, and ordered the stores which had already been put on shipboard to be detained. Du Coudray sailed alone on the 14th of February, 1776. Kalb resolved to wait a more favorable opportunity.

And now I have a story to tell which has lain hidden for near a century among the papers of Kalb, and was brought to light by the exhaustive researches of Mr. Kapp. It is a striking confirmation of the importance of the preservation of documents. At first blush it seems almost too strange to be believed. But the circumstances under which it was found leave no doubt of its authenticity. It throws so strong a light on the motives by which some, at least, of our foreign assistants were actuated, that I should do injustice to the reader were I to weaken it by abridgment.

" I have seen with pleasure," writes De Broglie at his country seat, Ruffec, the 11th of December, " from the relations of M. Dubois Martin, as well as from your last letter of the 5th instant, the good progress of your affairs, and hope that all your wishes will continue to be realized. You may rest assured that, on my part, I shall not neglect your interests, which, as you will not fail to remember, I have at all times advocated, the more cheerfully that I know that the favor of the king could not be better bestowed.

" I do not doubt that the plan communicated to you by M. Dubois meets your entire approbation. It is clearly indispensable to the permanence of the work. A military and political

leader is wanted, — a man fitted to carry the
weight of authority in the colony, to unite its
parties, to assign to each his place, to attract a
large number of persons of all classes and carry
them along with him, not courtiers, but brave,
efficient, and well educated officers, who confide
in their superior and repose implicit faith in him.
There need not be many grades of a higher
order ; but there is need of some, because the
corps and the country are separate from each
other. Not but what there is room enough for
a number of persons from among whom a selection may be made. The main point of the mission with which you have been intrusted will
therefore consist in explaining the advantage,
or rather the absolute necessity, of the choice of
a man who would have to be invested with the
power of bringing his assistants with him and
of assigning to each the position for which he
should judge him to be fitted. The rank of the
candidate would have to be of the first eminence ;
such, however, would have to be confined to the
army, excluding the civil service, with perhaps
the single exception of the political negotiations
with foreign powers. In proposing such a man,
you must of course not appear to know whether
he entertains any wish for such a position ; but
at the same time you must intimate that nothing but the most favorable stipulations would in-

duce him to make the sacrifices expected of him. You would have to observe that three years would be the longest period for which he could possibly bind himself, that he would claim a fixed salary, to continue after the expiration of that period of service, and that on no account would he consent to expatriate himself forever. What should make you particularly explicit on this point is, that the assurance of the man's return to France at the end of three years will remove every apprehension in regard to the powers to be conferred, and will remove even the semblance of an ambitious design to become the sovereign of the new republic.

" You will therefore content yourself with stipulating for a military authority for the person in question, who would unite the position of a general and president of the council of war with the title of generalissimo, field marshal, etc.

" Of course, large pecuniary considerations would have to be claimed for the preparations for the journey, and for the journey itself, and a liberal salary for the return home, much in the same way as has been done in the case of Prince Ferdinand. You can give the assurance that such a measure will bring order and economy into the public expenses, that it will reimburse its cost a hundred fold in a single campaign, and that the choice of officers who follow their leader

at his word, and from attachment to his person,
is worth more than the reinforcement of the
army with ten or twenty thousand men. You
well know the persons who adhere to this leader,
and the unlimited number of subalterns ; you
know that they are not courtiers, but excellent
and well tried soldiers ; you know better than
others the great difference between the one candidate and the other, and will lay particular
stress upon this point. You will be equally
mindful to dwell upon the effect necessarily produced by such an appointment on its mere an-
nouncement in Europe. Even in a good European army, everything depends upon the selection
of a good commander-in-chief ; how much more
in a cause where everything has yet to be created
and adjusted ! It is not easy to find a man qual-
ified for such a task, and at the same time willing
to undertake it. If matters down there — ' là
bas ' — should turn out well, you should induce
Congress to send immediately little Dubois back
to Mr. Deane, with full powers and directions.
These powers should be limited in no respect,
except in so far as to remove all danger of a too
extensive exercise of the civil authority or of
ambitious schemes for dominion over the republic. The desire is to be useful to the republic in
a political and military way, but with all the
appropriate honors, dignities, and powers over

subordinate functionaries; in short, with a well-ordered power.

" If you send back little Dubois, advise me at the same time of the true condition of affairs and of the state of public feeling, adding your suggestions of what is best to be done. Also inform me of the nature of the power conferred upon the agents of the insurgents. Farewell! I wish you and your caravan a pleasant journey. I shall execute your commissions, and shall see M. de Sartiges, when I get to Paris.

" Acquaint me with the receipt of this letter, and with the moment of your departure, and write to me under the direction of Abbé St. Evrard, at the bureau of M. St. Julien, treasurer general of the clergy. I leave this unsigned. You know who I am."

It is hard to say how far Kalb shared in the delusion of his patron. His knowledge of the colonies was the result of personal intercourse, and is so correct in most particulars that it seems impossible that he could have fallen into so great an error upon so important a point as their willingness to put a foreigner at the head of their government. The visions of power and wealth and glory which dazzled the eyes of De Broglie can hardly have disturbed the imagination of the cool-headed and deliberate German. Yet Silas

Deane, fresh from Congress, believed that the young nation, distrustful of its actual leaders, would gladly put a general of approved skill at its head. The affair of Du Coudray soon taught him better, and when Kalb reached Philadelphia, and saw what grave dissatisfaction the introduction of foreigners into places of trust and authority awakened, he shut up in his portfolio the record of his patron's ignorance and presumption. The secret, so wounding to the French general's vanity, was well kept, and no attempt was made to carry out the foolish and impracticable scheme.

The closing days of 1776 were not favorable to the American cause in France. None but the bad news from the American army had reached Europe. The brilliant movements on Trenton and Princeton were unknown, and the American cause, if not desperate, was looked upon as too doubtful to justify so bold an intervention as the transmission of arms in French bottoms, even though it was ostensibly made for the service of the French colonies. Lord Stormont's remonstrances were loud and apparently successful. Kalb returned to Paris to await a more auspicious moment.

His name now becomes intimately associated with the name of Lafayette. It was a profitable union for both. Kalb had age, experience, and

practical knowledge ; Lafayette, wealth, high
rank, and the ardor and enthusiasm of youth.
Both had firmness of purpose and strong wills.
For them the expedition possessed a singular
charm : the charm of generous sympathy and romantic adventure for the young man, of military
distinction and honorable activity for the old.
They resolved that the temporary delay should
not prevent them from carrying out their plan.
Lafayette had serious obstacles to apprehend
from the opposition of his family, especially from
that of his father-in-law, the Duke d'Ayen.   At
his request, in fact, rather than from any political
considerations, the ardent young nobleman was
ordered to renounce his project and travel in Italy
with his family.   In a conversation with the
Comte de Broglie, in which Kalb and the count's
secretary, Dubois Martin, took a part, it was
resolved that Lafayette should buy and freight a
ship, and sail without delay for the colonies, Kalb
and eleven officers accompanying him.   Kalb's
letters to his wife contain a minute history of the
embarrassments, both small and great, which delayed their embarkation.   At length, on the 20th
of April, they sailed, and on the 13th of June
made land on the coast of South Carolina.

It may not be undeserving of remark that
Lafayette, one of the earliest of abolitionists,
should have been brought for the first time into

contact with slavery on his first landing in the
country in which he first fought the battles of
freedom. The captain was out in his reckoning
and did not know where he was. Lafayette and
Kalb, with one of their companions and seven
sailors, took to the boat and rowed towards the
shore to look for a pilot. The first persons they
met were three negro oystermen, who could only
tell them that they belonged to a major in the
American army, and that the coast was infested
by hostile cruisers. The negroes guided them to
their master's house. They reached it about
ten in the evening, and were received with characteristic hospitality. There was much to ask and
to tell. Huger, for that was the major's name,
told the progress of the war. Kalb and Lafayette
could speak of the public sentiment in France, to
which American eyes were turned with such deep
anxiety. It was an auspicious beginning of their
adventurous career.

From Huger's hospitable mansion they pro-
ceeded to Charleston, where their ship had already arrived, and, disposing profitably of the
cargo, hastened towards Philadelphia with as
much speed as the heat of July would permit.
The day after their arrival they presented themselves at the door of Congress; and now, for the
first time, they saw what trouble Deane had
caused by his unauthorized promises of rank and

high pay to foreigners. Du Coudray's position was still equivocal, and here was a new body to provide for, three of them major-generals. The president of Congress referred them to Mr. Lovell, chairman of the committee of foreign affairs, who, receiving their letters and recommendations, told them that Congress had refused to ratify the agreements made by Mr. Deane. They had come at an unfortunate moment. Du Coudray's arrogant claims had raised a general ferment of indignation. Congress was fast losing the confidence of the army. Greene, Knox, and Sullivan had offered their resignations. Would it be just or even safe to accept them, and fill their places with foreigners? Congress resolved to make the best of its awkward position. It was resolved that the officers for whom no provision could be made should have their expenses paid, and return home. Lafayette asked to be allowed to serve as a volunteer and without pay. He had brought private letters from Franklin, as well as Deane, which called attention to the moral strength which his name would give to the American cause in France. His prayer was granted, and he received the commission of major-general. But his generous nature did not allow him to stop here. He felt himself drawn towards Kalb by a sense of gratitude, and a conviction that the services of the experienced soldier would be very

useful to the half-trained army of the new republic. He resolved to use all his influence
to secure them, and assured his friend that he
would not accept his own commission unless one
of equal rank should be given to him. With
equal generosity Kalb refused the offer, and advised the young general to join the army without delay.

The position of Congress was a difficult one,
even for very wise men. To ratify Deane's contracts would be not only to offend their own officers, and through them their immediate constitu-
ents, but, what could not be done without danger,
it would put the most important positions in the
army in the hands of foreigners, who had no other
interest in the contest than that of pay and rank.
The contracts, on the other hand, were technic-
ally binding, and if brought before a court would
be decided against the Congress. Another point
also required their careful consideration. Without
the aid and sympathy of France it would be impossible for them to obtain arms and military
stores in the quantity which their needs required.
The commerce with England, whence the colonies had drawn their annual supplies for house and
home, was broken off, and they looked to that of
France and Spain for a compensation. To send a
body of discontented officers home to tell in every
coffee-house that the young nation had begun its

career by violating a solemn contract would have
dulled the edge of sympathy and excited the sus-
picions of commerce. The discarded officers took
their disappointment to heart, and even the cool
and judicious Kalb gave vent to his indignation
in a bitter letter to the president of Congress.
But bitterly as Kalb felt on this occasion, he had
seen too much of the world not to feel that Congress was substantially in the right, and that an
army commanded by foreigners would be a dangerous foundation to build upon in a civil war.
In a letter to his wife, to whom he seems to
have communicated all his thoughts and feelings
with the utmost confidence, he acknowledges that
" his company was too numerous and invested
with too many positions of a high grade not to
have excited the natural discontent of the American officers."   In this dangerous dilemma Congress took the wisest course, disavowed Deane,
and assumed the expenses of the rejected officers. Kalb was employed to arrange and present their accounts, which were accepted and
promptly paid.

Meanwhile the shrewd diplomatist had not
passed so many weeks in Philadelphia in vain.
Part of the time, it is true, he was confined to a
sick bed, but even that was a means of bringing
him into personal contact with some of the leading members of government. No one could con-

verse with him often without being convinced of his fine parts, extensive observation, and sound judgment. As these gentlemen compared their observations, they became convinced that Kalb was too valuable a man to be rejected. Accordingly Congress resolved to appoint another major-general, and offered the commission to him, with the same date as that of Lafayette. The offer found him at Bethlehem, where he was making a visit to his Moravian brethren. His first impulse was to reject it, for he did not know in what light his acceptance would be looked upon by his patrons, the De Broglies, and the officers who had accompanied him. Further reflection convinced him that there was no good reason for a refusal. On the 13th of October he set out for the army.

He was welcomed by the officers as a brother in arms. Conway alone, who was already engaged in the infamous cabal which bears his name, looked coldly upon him, complaining that Kalb had been his inferior in France and could not justly be allowed to outrank him here. But Conway was already well known in the army, and little importance was attached to his opinion, although in Congress he had friends enough to procure him the coveted promotion, even in direct opposition to the avowed wishes of Washington. Kalb's story now becomes closely interwoven with the story of the war. He was sent in November, with St. Clair and Knox, to examine the fortifications of Red Bank, by which Washington still hoped to starve Howe out of Philadelphia. He was present at the council of war which was called to decide upon the propriety of an attack upon Philadelphia, and voted with the majority against it. Fortunately for the historian he was as fond of his pen as of his sword, and his minute and frequent letters to his wife and the Comte de Broglie are full of history, and valuable not merely as a record of events but of opinions. It was some time before he was able to form a correct idea of Washington. His personal qualities he was struck with at once; but the campaign of '77 had not been a brilliant one, and mistakes had been made which he erroneously laid at the door of the commander-in-chief. "I have not yet told you anything of the character of General Washington," he writes to the Comte de Broglie, on the 24th of September. "He is the most amiable, kind-hearted and upright of men; but as a general he is too indolent, too slow, and far too weak; besides he has a tinge of vanity in his composition, and overestimates himself. In my opinion, whatever success he may have will be owing to good luck and to the blunders of his adversaries rather than to his abilities. I may even say that he does not know how to

improve even upon the grossest blunders of the
enemy. He has not yet overcome his old prejudices against the French." This language sounds
strangely as applied to Washington; yet it is
historically important to know that it was actually used. If we inquire when, we shall find
that it was at the time of the Conway cabal, when
Washington's enemies were bold and loud, although there is no reason to suppose that Kalb
was in any way connected with them.

A few weeks later his opinion is materially
modified. "He is the bravest and truest of men,"
he writes, "has the best intentions and a sound
judgment. I am convinced that he would accomplish substantial results if he would only act
more upon his own responsibility; but it is a pity
that he is so weak and has the worst of advisers
in the men who enjoy his confidence." He had
already written: "It is unfortunate that Washington is so easily led." This is nearly the language of Lee and Reed a year before. They had
all mistaken for want of decision the self-distrust
which arose from a consciousness of inexperience.
It was not long before Kalb's opinion was still
farther modified. "He must be a very modest
man. . . . . He did and does more every day than
could be expected from any general in the world
in the same circumstances, and I think him the
only proper [person (nobody actually being or

serving in America excepted), by his natural and acquired capacity, his bravery, good sense, uprightness, and honesty, to keep up the spirits of the army and people, and I look upon him as the sole defender of his country's cause. Thus much I thought myself obliged to say on that head. I only could wish, in my private opinion, he would take more upon himself, and trust more to his own excellent judgment than to councils." This language was a decided renunciation of the schemes of De Broglie. "If I return to Europe," he writes to the count himself, "it will be with the greatest mortification, as it is impossible to execute the great design I have so gladly come to subserve. M. de Valfort will tell you that the project in question is totally impracticable: it would be regarded no less as an act of crying injustice towards Washington, than as an outrage on the honor of the country."

Kalb was with the army during its last operations before Philadelphia, and its bleak winter encampment at Valley Forge. He was restless and dissatisfied. Among his many hard experiences this was the hardest. His judgment as a scientific soldier was offended. His aspirations for military distinction were thwarted. He longed for the well clad and thoroughly disciplined armies with which he had fought under Saxe and against Frederick. He pours out his

soul to his wife and his friend, and there was a
great deal of bitterness in it. Like all his letters,
those of this period are full of materials for history. He writes with freedom of acts and opinions, often using strong expressions, though seldom speaking of persons by name. He condemns
in unmeasured terms the choice of encampment,
saying that none but an enemy of the commander-in-chief could have advised him to risk his
army in such a position. His picture of camp-
life is almost a satire. He hardly seems to know
how to speak of the love for titles which makes
every man a colonel; or of the love of display
which wearied the troops with unprofitable parades, and led officers of every grade to strip the
ranks in order to secure a full array of unnecessary servants. The expense of living he finds
enormous, and believes that many bills are paid
which will not bear examination. "I am the
only general," he writes, "who practices economy. Nevertheless, at the last camp I had to
pay my purveyor of milk and butter two hundred and forty-two francs for the consumption of
two weeks." He does not know what his pay is,
whether a hundred and fifty dollars a month or
two hundred, but whichever it may be it will be
paid in paper and subjected to a discount of
four hundred per cent. before he can get silver
for it. The contractors make, he has no doubt,

10

fifty per cent. on their contracts; and throughout the whole department of supplies he finds a dangerous spirit of peculation. Nothing, however, gives him greater pain than the jealousies and bickerings of the French officers. Few as they comparatively were, they were divided into parties, and embittered against each other by an intolerant party spirit. The only exception was Lafayette, who, attaching himself to Washington, seemed to have no other view than the success of the cause to which he had dedicated his fortune and life. "I always meet him," Kalb writes, "with the same cordiality and the same pleasure. He is an excellent young man, and we are good friends. It were to be wished that all the Frenchmen who serve here were as reasonable as he and I. Lafayette is much liked; he is on the best of terms with Washington; both of them have every reason to be satisfied with me also." With Greene and Knox he does not seem to have formed any close association, even if he did not go further and avoid them as Washington's evil counselors.

Be this as it may, the winter at Valley Forge was a trying winter to Kalb. He could not adapt himself to American camp life, and, what tried him yet more, he could not see those prospects of laurels in it which had been his chief aim in coming to America. Then came rumors of European wars, and visions of honors won under his old commander, De Broglie, began to float before his dazzled eyes. Then his diplomatic ambition was awakened, and he thought it would be a pleasant thing to be the French envoy to Congress, or to represent France in Protestant Geneva. Sometimes, also, while he wrote to his wife, he longed for more tranquil scenes and a purer happiness; he would throw up his commission and go home to live with her and their children. Dreams, all of them. The weeks and months passed on, and every day the fetters which his ambition had forged grew firmer.

But the winter was not altogether an inactive one. It was the winter of the Conway cabal, and Kalb's good sense led him to the side of Washington. From the Conway cabal sprang the expedition to Canada, framed solely to detach Lafayette from the commander-in-chief. The snare was avoided by Lafayette's insisting upon Kalb instead of Conway for the second in command. When the two generals reached Albany, they found that no preparations had been made for the opening of the campaign; neither men nor stores had been collected. It was too late to begin, and they returned to camp. During this fruitless expedition Kalb was brought more directly into collision with Conway, who, claiming to have outranked him in France, claimed not to be outranked by him here.

Meanwhile came the tidings of the French alliance, which seemed to make the victory of the Americans sure. They were received in camp with great exultation, and a day set apart for public rejoicing. On this occasion Kalb commanded the centre, and Lafayette the left wing. A council of war was called to decide how this accession of a great ally could be made available. "But for the late treaty," Kalb writes to his wife on the 25th of May, 1778, "I should have returned to you ere this. Now I cannot and will not do it for various reasons, two of which I shall here specify. In the first place, war between England and France having become inevitable, should I fall into the hands of the English while at sea my treatment would be that of a French prisoner of war, possibly without a claim to being exchanged, inasmuch as I should have left America without leave from my own government. In the second place, the alliance with the United States transforms me from an officer on two years' furlough into a general of the French army, with the same, if not a better, title to promotion than if I had never quitted France. Henceforward, therefore, I shall only return by express command of the minister."

Kalb was one of those who thought the contest virtually ended by the alliance with France. "Since France has interfered in the war," he writes to his wife, on the 7th of October, "the subjugation of the continent by the English is out of the question. Possibly they will even surrender Rhode Island, New York, Long Island, and Staten Island, to defend their own country and their remaining colonies. At all events, there will be no more movements of importance. I therefore regard the war as ended, as far as I am concerned, having no disposition to do battle against the savages on the frontier." But his conjecture was not realized. It was not merely her rebellious colonies that were in arms against England, but her rival and natural enemy, France. The same narrow policy which had cost so much blood and treasure was desperately clung to in this day of trial and danger, and although there could be but one end to such a war, she declared war against France. For four more campaigns Kalb remained with the army, sharing all its hardships, but by a singular fatality not being present at any of its battles. Among its hardships was that of the second winter encampment at Morristown, when the ice in the Hudson was six feet thick, and cavalry and heavy ordnance went from New York to Staten Island on it. These were not the laurels which Kalb had left his pleasant home and beautiful wife to win.

His patience was sorely tried. " As often as a Frenchman returns home," he writes to his wife, " my heart is ready to burst with homesickness." New campaigns come and go monotonously. I shall not follow his steps in detail, but content myself with gathering a few side lights to bring out the characteristic points of my picture more faithfully.

" What I am doing here," he writes to his wife on the 15th of July, " is extremely disagreeable. Without my excellent constitution, it would be impossible to bear up long under this service. Yesterday I made the most wearisome trip of my life, visiting the posts and pickets of the army in the solitudes, woods, and mountains, clambering over the rocks, and picking my way in the most abominable roads. My horse having fallen lame, I had to make the whole distance on foot. I never suffered more from heat. On my return I had not a dry rag on me, and was so tired that I could not sleep. My temperate and simple habits greatly contribute to keep me in good health. My general health is very good, and I hardly notice the annoyances of camp life. Dry bread and water make my breakfast and supper; at dinner I take some meat. I drink nothing but water, never coffee, and rarely chocolate or tea, in order to avoid irritating my eyes, which are the more useful to me as my four aids, partly from ignorance and partly from laziness, leave the writing incident to the service unattended to. So I am compelled to do it all myself, while they cultivate their digestions. I have now no more earnest wish than soon to see you and the children again, and never to leave you more. If our separation is destined to be of any advantage to us, it is dearly paid for."

Earnest as this longing for home unquestionably was, it may well be doubted whether a few weeks of domestic repose would not have brought back his yearning for active life.

ποθέεσκε δ᾽ ἀϋτήν τε πτόλεμόν τέ.

For well he loved clamor and combat.

He bears emphatic testimony to the barbarity with which the war was carried on on the part of the enemy. The English peace commissioners had threatened it when they saw that their mission had failed, and Sir Henry Clinton did not scruple to put the threat in execution. "General Clinton," Kalb writes, "having left a garrison in New York, is amusing himself with plundering, burning, and ravaging. Fairfield, Bedford, Norwalk, New Haven, and West Haven have already felt his rage. The mode of warfare here practiced is the most barbarous that could be conceived; whatever the enemy cannot carry off in their forays is destroyed or burned. They

cannot possibly triumph in the end.   Their cruelty and inhumanity. must sooner or later draw
down upon their heads the vengeance of Heaven,
and blast a government which authorizes these
outrages."   Such words from an officer who had
gone through the Seven Years' War, and seen
with his own eyes the inhumanity with which it
was waged, afford a strong confirmation of the
charges which the Americans brought against the
English.

We have seen that there was a great mystery
hanging over Kalb's education.   From this point
of view the following passage has a peculiar
interest.   " Yesterday," he writes in the letter
from which I last quoted, " I was reconnoitring
all day in the vicinity of my post, of course on
foot; I must repeat the same operation forthwith,
in order to be familiar with my position by dinner time. . . . . Though very tired I have already
returned from my excursion," he continues at four
o'clock of the same day, " and I have just dined.
The staff officers of my division were my guests.
We were all very hungry, and did full justice to
the mutton and beef which constituted the re-
past; large round crackers served as plates in the
absence of any kind of crockery.   The scene
forcibly reminded me of the conquest of Italy by
Æneas, and the words of Ascanius, when they
had reached the future site of Rome.   There,

too, hunger compelled them to devour the cakes upon which their food had been served up, and recalled the oracle of the harpies, that they would not reach the end of their wanderings and toils, nor call Italy theirs, until they should have eaten their tables with their meals. I have, unfortunately, no Ascanius with me, but I desire most ardently that my fate may be decided as was that of Æneas, that the independence of America, like the conquest of Italy, may now be realized, and that, after we too have eaten our tables, the close of our warfare and toils may be likewise approaching."

It is pleasant to find a burst of enthusiasm in so deliberate a man as Kalb. A letter from Washington, announcing the capture of Stony Point, came while his party was still at table. "I drank no wine," he writes, "as the others did, yet I was carried away by the same enthusiasm. I called Mr. Jacob, and told him to bring me a bottle of champagne. He stared at me with astonishment, saying he had none. 'Then there must be some port wine at least?' 'That is on the baggage wagons.' I apologized for my defective memory, and was sorry to have tantalized the company with delusive hopes; but they were satisfied to take my good will for the deed. I promised all my guests to give them the best of champagne at Paris, and shall be delighted to keep my word."

We meet another trait, in these letters, worth remembering : " The taking of Stony Point forms an epoch in the history of the war of American independence, because it was on this occasion that our troops first ventured to attack the intrenchments of the enemy, and because they displayed great valor in doing so. The action lasted only twenty-five minutes. A hundred or a hundred and twenty of the British were killed and wounded, while we had thirty killed and sixty wounded. I mean to tell the truth, in spite of what the newspapers will say about our losses, greatly exaggerating, of course, the number of the fallen foe, and cutting down our own casualties. But I am unable to appreciate the subtlety of this system of lies told by everybody and believed by no one, and prefer to comfort myself with the well tried proverb, ' On ne fait point d'omelette sans casser des œufs.' " (You cannot make an omelet without breaking some eggs.)

From the French alliance to the spring of 1780, Kalb was constantly with the army, sharing all its hardships, cold, hunger, fatigue, the nights on a camp-stool or on the bare ground, clothes falling about him in rags, and his ink freezing in his pen as he writes close by the fire. He resolves to go to Philadelphia to buy clothes. He has to pay four hundred dollars for a hat, for a pair of boots the same, and other things in proportion.

He wants a good horse, but is asked a price
equivalent to ten years of his pay, and therefore
falls back on his old stock. His letters to his
wife are filled with interesting details, some of
them not very creditable to the public spirit of
the times. His division was composed of one regiment from Delaware and seven from Maryland,
divided into two brigades, the first under Smallwood and all Marylanders, the second under Gist,
and containing three Maryland and one Delaware regiment; two thousand and thirty men in
all. From time to time some of the States sent
their officers supplies of a kind which could not
be found in the market, coffee, cognac, tea, and
sugar. As commanding officer, Kalb would be
entitled to a share, but Smallwood, violating both
the laws of military subordination and the laws
of good breeding, set a watch over them to prevent any of them from going into the hands of
Kalb, who, he said, not being a Marylander, had
no right to them. Fortunately not all of our
officers were so churly or so ignorant of the pro-
prieties of life.

"My march," he writes to a German friend
from Petersburg, Virginia, when on his way to
reinforce the southern army, "my march costs
me enormous sums. I cannot travel with my
equipage, I am therefore compelled to resort to
inns. My six months' earnings will scarce defray

the most indispensable outlay of a single day.
Not long since I was compelled to take a night's
lodging at a private house. For a bed, supper,
and grog for myself, my three companions, and
three servants I was charged, on going off without a breakfast next day, the sum of eight hundred and fifty dollars. The lady of the house
politely added that she had charged nothing for
the rooms, and would leave the compensation for
them to my discretion, although three or four
hundred dollars would not be too much for the
inconvenience to which she had been put by myself and my followers." No wonder that he
should add, " And these are the people who talk
of sacrificing their all in the cause of liberty."

I give these details with reluctance, but I feel
myself bound to give them, because they are a
part of the history of the times. Those who look
upon the history of our war of independence as
an unqualified history of generous sacrifices, take
a false view of the subject. Base and ignoble
passions manifested themselves by the side of the
noblest passions. Some men were always true,
as some were always false. We had but one
Arnold, but we had many lesser villains, who
played the spy on both sides, sometimes fought
on both sides, and grew rich by speculating upon
the necessities of their country. Our national
history, like the early history of Rome, has suffered greatly from apocryphal heroism.

Meanwhile a change had taken place in the strategy of the British general. Experience had shown the impossibility of conquering the Americans by the north. He resolved to carry the war into the south. Savannah was taken; siege was laid to Charleston. Lincoln, who was in command in the south, called earnestly for reinforcements; and, on the 3d of April, Kalb was ordered to march with his division to the succor of the besieged city. It was a long and weary march, during which men and officers were exposed to great hardships. It was an occasion, also, which called out Kalb's military and executive talents to the best advantage. Supplies of all kinds were wanted, and he hurried on to Philadelphia to urge upon Congress the necessity of employing all its authority in order to collect them. The means of transportation, in particular, were wanting. " Virginia promised them, but," he writes to his friend, Dr. Phyle of Philadelphia, " I meet with no support, no integrity, and no virtue in the State of Virginia, and place my sole reliance on the French fleet and army which are coming to our relief." With every step in advance his embarrassments increased. " What a difference between war in this country and in Europe," he writes to his wife. " Those who do not know the former know not what it is to contend against obstacles." At Petersburg he received the tidings of the fall of Charleston, an event which had been foreseen and provided for. The enemy had as yet no firm footing in the Carolinas, and he was to prevent them from gaining one. He presses on, his difficulties daily increasing, for the further he advanced the more difficult he found it to obtain wagons and food. North Carolina had prepared no supplies for the Union troops, reserving all her stores for the militia; a body utterly untrustworthy for a campaign of marches and countermarches, and which in North Carolina was deeply tainted with toryism. As chief in command, and consequently brought into frequent contact with dilatory legislatures and ignorant militia, Kalb had much to endure. He had physical trials also, hardly less annoying, which he describes to his wife in those long and frequent letters that give so pleasant a picture of his married life. "Here I am at last," he writes from Goshen, on the borders of North Carolina, "considerably south, suffering from intolerable heat and the worst of quarters, and the most voracious insects of every hue and form. The most disagreeable of the latter is what is commonly called the tick, a kind of strong black flea, which makes its way under the skin, and by its bite produces the most painful irritation and inflammation, which last a number of days. My whole body is covered with their stings."

One of his worst foes was hunger. Failing to obtain provisions from the State executive, he was compelled to send out foraging parties, a painful and yet an insufficient resource, for the farmers were living on the last year's crop, which was nearly exhausted, while the new crop, though full of promise to the eye, was not yet ripe; and although the commanders of these parties were ordered to treat the inhabitants with the greatest leniency, they could not but add materially to the miseries of the suffering country. When this resource failed, he was compelled to advance towards the richer districts.

It is only by minute details that such pictures as these can be made faithful, or such services as Kalb's be placed in their true light. Yet even in this hasty sketch there is enough to prove that he possessed some of the soldier's highest qualities in the highest degree. But we are near the end. On the 13th of July a letter from General Gates announces to Kalb that the command of the southern army has been transferred to the successful leader of the northern army of 1777. Kalb replies, on the 16th, from his camp on the Deep River, giving a concise description of his condition and prospects, and expressing his satisfaction at the promise of being relieved from so difficult a command. If anything could have prepared Gates's mind for a true conception of the condition of his army, it would have been an unvarnished tale like this. But his brain had been heated by success, and, fancying that the men who had turned a deaf ear to the representations of Kalb would act with energy and promptitude at the call of the favorite of Congress, he pushed on to Wilcox's Mills on the Deep River, where the famishing army lay encamped. Kalb received him with a salute of thirteen guns and all the pomp and circumstance that his scanty means would permit, and then sank, with a lightened heart, into the subordinate position of a commander of division. Gates paid him the compliment of confirming his standing orders, but startled officers and men by ordering them to hold themselves in readiness to set out, the next morning, on the direct route to Camden. When reminded in a written memorial, signed by all the leading officers, that the direct route led through a desolate and barren region, and that there was not food enough in camp for a single day, he replied that supplies of provisions and rum were on their way from the north, and would reach the army in two days at the furthest. " I have but to stamp my foot," said Pompey, " and armed men will start from the soil of Italy." " I have but to show myself," thought Gates, " and Cornwallis will take refuge in Charleston."

The disastrous march began. Disease, heat,

and hunger fought for the enemy. Mutiny was
twice at the door. Neither supplies nor reinforcements came. Molasses was used to temper the
brackish water. The meat was the meagre beef
of the pine barrens, in small quantities. For
bread they ate unripened corn and peaches still
half green. By the 13th of August they were
within thirteen miles of the enemy. On the
15th, the heavy baggage, camp equipage, the
sick, and women and children were sent to the
rear, and orders issued for a night march. A
council of war was called, not for consultation,
but to confirm the general's plan of action. The
confidence in his judgment had not been increased by the knowledge that he had estimated
his strength at 7000 men, when he had but 3052
fit for duty. The confidence in his tactics was
shaken when it was seen that, against all the laws
of tactics, he had placed at the head of a column
in a night march Armand's cavalry, a body of
raw and undisciplined foreigners. Kalb urged
that they should remain at Clermont, a place
strong by nature and capable of being made
stronger by art. This, too, he argued, was the
true course for the American army, the motley
composition of which was much better adapted
to defense than to attack; but this wise counsel
was not heeded. " We may have Cornwallis
against us," said an officer. " He will not dare

11

to look me in the face," was Gates's reply. " I wonder where we shall dine to-morrow," said another. " Dine, sir," was the answer, " why, where, but in Camden? I would n't give a pinch of snuff for the certainty of eating my breakfast at Camden to-morrow, and seeing Lord Cornwallis my guest at table."

At ten in the evening the tents were struck, and the troops, filing into position, began their march. The sky was clear, the stars shone brightly, but the air was sultry, and night had none of its wonted coolness to repair the strength consumed by the burning heat of the day. Silence was enjoined under penalty of death. The deep sand deadened the rumbling of the artillery and the heavy tread of the men. The air gleamed with myriads of fire-flies. But every now and then men sickened and fell out of the ranks. Meanwhile Cornwallis, little dreaming that his enemy was so near, was advancing at the head of 2233 men, in the hope of coming upon the Americans by surprise at Clermont. Thus the two armies were fast approaching each other, each ignorant of the proximity of his enemy. At about two in the morning they met in a glade in the pine forest which fell off with a gentle declination towards Saunder's Creek, about half a mile distant, and was covered on both flanks by impenetrable marshes; a position not wanting in

strength, but too narrow for the easy management of troops. A brisk fire followed the collision, and in the skirmish Armand's cavalry
was thrown back upon the first Maryland brigade,.
which caught the panic and broke. But Porter-
field's light infantry held its ground and drove
the English, though with the loss of their gallant leader. Both sides paused, and drawing a
little back, waited with throbbing hearts to see
what daylight might reveal.

From some prisoners, who had been taken
in the skirmish, Williams, the adjutant-general,
learned that Cornwallis himself was at the head
of the hostile army, and hastened with the intelligence to Gates. The inconsiderate general
could not conceal his amazement. "Let a council be called," was his comment upon the un-
welcome tidings. Williams hurried to Kalb.
"Well," said the veteran, "did not the commanding general immediately order a retreat?"
The council met in the rear of the American
lines. "You know our situation, gentlemen,"
said Gates, "what had we better do?" A deep
and ominous silence followed. Kalb had already
twice offered wise council which had been rejected. It was not in his nature to offer it again.
The first to speak was the impetuous Stevens.
"We must fight, gentlemen: it is not yet too
late: we can do nothing else, we must fight."

"We must fight then," said Gates. "Gentlemen, to your posts!"

At break of day the battle began. The first scene was soon ended. Unable to stand the fierce onset of Cornwallis's veterans, the Virginia militia broke and fled, carrying the North Carolinians with them in their headlong flight. "I will bring the rascals with me back into line," exclaimed Gates, and spurred after them, not stopping till he reached Charlotte, sixty miles from the field of battle. And now the interest centres in Kalb. The final hour of the veteran, who had fought under Saxe, and taken an honorable part in the Seven Years' War, was come in the last and only honorable hour of the battle of Camden. He had drawn up the army, putting himself at the head of the men of Delaware and Maryland. A dense fog hung over the battle-field, pressing the smoke so low that it was impossible to distinguish objects even at a small distance, and it was some time before he became aware of the flight of the left wing and centre. Then, gathering all his forces around him, conscious of his danger but not despairing of victory, he led them to the charge. It must have been a thrilling sight to see how firmly they held their ground, how they fired volley after volley into the enemy's ranks, how, when they had opened their way by their musketry, they fol-

lowed it up by the bayonet. Above them all tow-
ered the gallant German at their head. His
sword was stained deepest, his battle-cry rang
clearest; there was triumph in the keen flash of
his eye, if not the victor's triumph, the triumph of
duty done. Three times he led his willing men
to the charge. Three times they were forced
back by superior numbers. For numbers began
to tell. His horse was shot under him. His
head was laid open by a sabre stroke. Jaquette,
the adjutant of the Delaware regiment, bound up
the wound with his scarf and besought him to
withdraw from the fight. Without heeding the
appeal, Kalb led the charge on foot. Wound
followed wound, but he held his ground desperately. At last, concentrating his strength in a
final charge, Cornwallis came on. The Marylanders broke. Kalb fell, bleeding from eleven
wounds; still at this supreme moment strong
enough to cut down a soldier who was aiming his
bayonet at his breast. "The rebel general, the
rebel general!" shouted the enemy, as they
caught sight of his epaulettes. "Spare the
Baron de Kalb," cried his adjutant, Dubuysson,
vainly throwing himself upon his body and trying to shield it with his own from the thirsty
bayonets. He spoke to hearts hardened by the
fierce spirit of battle. The furious English
raised the helpless warrior from the ground, and

leaning him against a wagon began to strip him. At this moment Cornwallis and his suite rode up. They found him already stripped to his shirt and with the blood streaming from eleven wounds. "I regret to see you so badly wounded, but am glad to have defeated you," said the victorious general, and immediately gave orders that his brave antagonist should be properly cared for. For three days Kalb's strong frame struggled with death. Dubuysson watched by his bedside. English officers came to express their sympathy and regret. Soldier to the last, his thoughts were with the brave men who had faced the enemy so gallantly at his command, and just before he expired he charged his faithful adjutant to give them his "thanks for their valor, and bid them an affectionate farewell."

On the 19th' he died, — three days after the battle. The masons of the British army took part in his funeral, and buried him with masonic rites. Gates announced his death to Congress in terms of warm admiration; and Congress voted a monument to his memory which has never been erected. Till 1821, the solitary tree under which he had been buried was the only record of the spot where he lay. Then proposals were made to erect a monument to him at Camden, and after some delay the work was begun. Little progress had been made, when Lafayette's last visit to this country in 1825 revived, for a moment, the sense of local rather than of national obligation, and the illustrious Frenchman, who had been Kalb's first companion, was, with peculiar propriety, asked to lay the corner-stone of this tardy tribute to the memory of his heroic friend.

GERMAN MERCENARIES.

———◆———

Vende la carne loro, essendo viva.
He sells their flesh, it being yet alive.
DANTE, *Purgatorio*, xiv.

GERMAN MERCENARIES.

In the states of antiquity all citizens owed
military service to the state. During the Middle Ages this military relation assumed the
form of a personal obligation, which bound the
vassal to answer the call to arms of his liege
lord with a number of men proportioned to the
extent of the domain which he held of him.
When wars became longer and more expensive,
the sovereign found himself dependent upon the
good-will of his vassals for the success of his
arms. His right to command was unquestionable. The vassal, if dissatisfied, might disobey;
and thus the final question between them was a
question of power — of power to enforce, or of
power to rebel.

Among the more active of the German em-
perors whose aspirations exceeded their means of
action was Maximilian the First, known to his
contemporaries as Maximilian the Moneyless.
Though married to the powerful Mary of Bur-
gundy, he received no aid from her vassals;

though active and energetic, he was abandoned
by his own. The Swiss had fallen from him,
and he had neither the money to buy, nor the
strength to force them back. It was then, and
probably with no conception of the full significance of what he was doing, that, instead of ad-
dressing himself to his nobles as feudal vassals, he
raised an army of free burghers and peasants in
eastern Austria, Suabia, and the Tyrol. This
army was composed of infantry. Gunpowder
had already reduced the fully armed knight to
the level of the soldier on foot, or in other words
the contest between the noble and the plebeian,
which had been waged so long and so disastrously
in Rome, was renewed in modern Europe under
different circumstances and in a new form. It
was a war between industry and privilege, between mechanical skill, or physical power under
the control of an intelligent will, and brute
force ; a question, as time developed it, between
the longest purse and the longest sword. It is
no part of my present object to follow the progress of this contest from the first landsknechts
of Maximilian to the perfect machines of the
Great Frederick. I wish only to call attention
to the fact that the reinstatement of the infantry
to their true position soon opened the way for the
decline of the old feudal armies and the enlistment of troops for longer terms of service. He

who could pay best was surest of finding willing
soldiers. Commercial states like Venice could
always raise whatever sums they wanted at five
per cent., while Charles VIII. was checked in
the very beginning of his Italian wars and compelled to pay forty-two per cent. for the means
of continuing them. Thus new resources were
opened for the formation of armies. Princes
could carry on war as long as their subjects could
be made to pay for it, and war itself became a
lucrative and honored pursuit. From regular
bands of mercenaries came standing armies and
that oppressive military system of modern Europe which has weighed so heavily upon the la-
boring classes and retarded the moral, the intellectual, and the industrial development of society.
All the great wars of modern Europe, till the
wars of the French Revolution, had been carried on in a large measure by mercenary troops,
among which the Germans were perhaps the
foremost for aptitude to arms, power of endurance, cruelty, rapacity, and, as long as they were
regularly paid, for fidelity to their banner. But
no sooner did their pay fall in arrears than they
grew disobedient and discontented, and if not
bought over were presently found fighting and
plundering on the other side. Would you see
the mercenary in his perfect form, study the Captain Dalgetty of Scott's " Legend of Montrose,"

who cannot be induced by any temptation to enter upon new service until he has fulfilled all the conditions of the old ; who loves his horse, and grooms and feeds him before he provides for himself, yet who, when the faithful animal is killed, skins him with his own hands. But Dalgetty was an officer, and the distinction between officer and soldier was sharply drawn. For the officer there was promotion and social position. He embraced arms as a profession because he preferred them to any other profession. Of the political questions connected with war he knew and cared little. Of the moral question connected with it he knew and cared nothing. He was trained to look unmoved upon human suffering. The battle-field and hospital seldom appealed to his sympathies, for habit had blunted them. To fight and attract the eye of his commander was his ambition. To win a ribbon or a cross was his highest aspiration. If he were a captain, he might become a colonel. If he were a colonel, he might become a brigadier. And when peace came, there were Paris and garrisons to lounge and be idle in.

In these rewards the soldier of the ranks had no part. To be an officer required a nobility of four descents, and the private, once enlisted, became a mere machine in the hands of his superiors. But let us study this victim of a barbarous usage somewhat more in detail, for it is only by getting close to a subject that we can form a correct idea of it. These details bring into strong relief the difference between the present and the past, enabling us to measure for ourselves the progress and the effects of civilization. It is in the lessons drawn from this thorough comprehension of the past that the instruction of history lies, and among these lessons there is none truer than that institutions, like men, have their periods of strength and weakness, of growth and decay. The formation of regular troops was the beginning of a great revolution, which, while it strengthened the hands of the prince, opened new fields for the intellectual and moral growth of the peasant : not intentionally, indeed, but because human events obey subtle laws, and results often cover much broader ground than we think of in directing our aim.

When regular armies had taken the place of feudal armies, and military adventurers were ready to sell their own blood and that of their followers to the best paymaster, the question most urgent upon them all was how to fill their ranks and keep them full. Some were found who took service readily of their own accord. These were chiefly either middle-aged men, whom the habits of the camp had unfitted for any other kind of life, or young men easily dazzled by the splen dor of military display. They formed, however, but the skeleton of an army. Many more were wanted to fill its ranks. Of the cunning, the guile, the fraud, the heartless inhumanity with which the nefarious art of recruiting was carried on, we should find it impossible to form any idea had not the story been often told in forms which leave no room for doubt. We will borrow one of these dark pages from the Frederick of Mr. Carlyle.[1]

"All countries, especially all German countries, are infested with a new species of predatory two-legged animals — Prussian recruiters. They glide about, under disguise if necessary; lynx-eyed, eager almost as the Jesuit hounds are; not hunting the souls of men as the spiritual Jesuits do, but their bodies, in a merciless, carnivorous manner. Better not be too tall in any country at present! Irishmen could not be protected by the ægis of the British constitution itself. Generally, however, the Prussian recruiter on British ground reports that the people are too well off; that there is little to be done in those parts. . . . . Germany, Holland, Switzerland, the Netherlands, these are the fruitful fields for us, and there we do hunt with some vigor.

"For example, in the town of Jülich there lived and worked a tall young carpenter. One day, a

---

[1] *Life of Frederick II.*, book v. ch. 5.

well-dressed positive-looking gentleman (Baron
von Hompesch, the records namehim) enters the
shop; wants 'a stout chest with lock on it, for
household purposes; must be of such and such
dimensions, six feet six in length especially, and
that is an indispensable point—in fact, it will be
longer than yourself, I think, Herr Zimmer-
mann; what is the cost? when can it be ready?'
Cost, time, and the rest are settled. 'A right
stout chest, then; and see you don't forget the
size; if too short it will be of no use to me,
mind!' 'Ja wohl! Gewiss!' and the positive-
looking gentleman goes his ways. At the appointed day he reappears; the chest is ready;
we hope, an unexceptionable article. 'Too short,
as I had dreaded,' says the positive gentleman.
' Nay, your honor,' says the carpenter, 'I am certain it is six feet six,' and takes out his foot-rule.
' Pshaw! it was to be longer than yourself.'
' Well, it is.' ' No it is n't.' The carpenter, to
end the matter, gets into his chest and will convince any and all mortals. No sooner is he in,
rightly flat, than the positive gentleman, a Prussian recruiting officer in disguise, slams down
the lid upon him, locks it, whistles in three stout
fellows, who pick up the chest, gravely walk
through the streets with it, open it in a safe
place, and find — horrible to relate — the poor
carpenter dead! "

12

Once enlisted, how were recruits to be got safely to the camp or the garrison where they were to be converted into machines? The instructions framed for the guidance of the men entrusted with this difficult task will tell us. The first and most important point was to secure the safety of the recruiting officer charged with their transportation.   He was to be provided with good side-arms, always carry a pistol, and never allow the recruit to walk behind him, or come near enough to him to seize him by the body. And to give additional force to the precaution, the recruit was told that the first false step would cost him his life. If practicable, the recruiting officer in choosing a route was to avoid the province where his recruit had served before, or was born. He was to avoid also all large cities and prosperous villages.   In choosing quarters for the night he was to give the preference to inns frequented by recruiting officers, and where the landlord was on their side.   Even here the most watchful foresight was required.   The recruit was made to undress by word of command, and the clothes both of the officer and the recruit were handed to the landlord for safe-keeping over night.   The officer slept between the recruit and the door.

On the march the recruit must not be allowed to look about him, or stop, much less converse with passers-by, and particularly in a foreign language. The officer guides the recruit as you would guide a horse. The words halt, march, slow, fast, right, left, forward, must be obeyed on the instant; the slightest hesitation would be a bad omen for the authority of the officer. At the inns where they stopt overnight they were put, if possible, in an upper room, with iron bars to the windows. On no account could the recruit be allowed to leave the room overnight. A lamp was kept burning all night long, and close by an unlighted one must be ready for immediate use.

To prevent the recruit from seizing the officer's arms in the night, they were given to the landlord, as his clothes were, for safe-keeping; and in the morning, when they were given back, they were examined anew and the priming freshened. When he, the officer, is dressed and armed, he orders the recruit to rise and dress. In entering an inn or a room, the recruit goes first; in going out, last. In the inn itself, the officer sits in front of the table, the recruit behind it. If the recruit has a wife she is subject to the same laws which govern his motions, obeys the same word of command, and never walks before her husband; but in every way is made to feel that the eye of the vigilant guard is constantly upon her.

Care, too, is taken, on the route, to cut off the recruit from all communication with anybody but his guard. He must not be allowed pen or ink

or paper or pencil.   To prevent him from rising
upon his guard by the way, all his dangerous
weapons, even to a large knife, are taken away,
and neither he nor his wife is allowed the use of
a cane.   As with a novice among the Jesuits, all
his gestures and words are noted down and reported, with the remarks and comments of the
reporter.   If he actually makes an attempt to
escape, he must be instantly put in irons, or
have the thumb-screw put on him.   It is a bad
affair if the officer is under the necessity of using
his weapons and wounding or killing the recruit.

Care must be taken, also, that the recruit be
not an over match for his guard.   Every stout,
well-built, bold-faced recruit must be closely
watched, and it may even become necessary to
double the guard.   The danger of escape pre-
sents itself in lively forms to the imagination of
the author of the instructions.   He calculates cau-
tiously how many recruiting officers may be required for a given number of recruits, and comes
to the conclusion that under the most favorable
circumstances three officers may take charge of
seven or even nine recruits.

" But two recruits should never be entrusted
to one officer.   Should this, however, seem to be
unavoidable, it is extremely unfortunate for the
officer.   When it is absolutely impossible for the
officer to keep the recruits back till he becomes

strong enough to give them a proper guard, he must hire somebody to help him. It is better to incur expense for the sake of foresight, than to injure the recruit or expose the life of the officer to inevitable danger." The tone of regret in this last sentence reminds us that it was not awakened by apprehension for the loss of a human being, but from fear that a name might be stricken from the muster-roll. One more provision completes the picture. "For the recruiting officer, and even more for his subordinate, a good dog will be very useful. He must be taught not to allow recruits to carry sticks in their hands; to bark if he sees one rise or move in the night; to drive him back if he sees one leave the road; to seize him if he sees him run, and only let go of him at his master's command; not to allow him to pick up anything, and many other precautions which may serve to lighten the task of the officer and his subaltern.

"And finally, if in passing a crowd or a city, the recruit should make a desperate attempt to escape by calling for help and declaring that he has been forced to enlist, the officer is directed to appeal to the authorities, who, after seeing his papers, will doubtless give him the necessary aid."

Suppose now that this watchfulness has been successful, that the recruit has been safely con-

veyed to the camp or garrison where he is to take
the first steps in this passage from a man to a
machine. Handcuffs, thumb-screws, heavy chains,
and, above all, the cane in strong hands, break
in'time the strongest will; repeated humiliations
destroy self-respect; familiarity with scenes of
violence and barbarity undermines the moral
sense; the recruit has no motive but to escape
punishment, and no comforter but the brandy
bottle. Yet even in these ashes live some sparks
of humanity, some of those sympathies which,
perhaps, are never altogether extinguished in the
human breast. Daily association in the same
duties, daily gatherings under the same flag,
awaken a certain sense of common interest and
feeling, and supply in a certain measure the human necessity of love. Whatever of pride is left
him centres in his flag. Such was the training
of the men who were hired to fight against the
Declaration of Independence. What mattered it
to them whether they fought in Germany or in
America, for a prince or for a people? If one
wishes to form a vivid conception of these
wretched men, looking straight into the picture,
he should read some of the scenes in George
Sand's "Consuelo," and Thackeray's "Memoirs
of Barry Lyndon." If one wishes to take the no-
bler point of view and look down upon the picture, he should read the life of Baron Riedesel

and the memoirs of his wife. And now for the bearings of this sketch upon American history.

It soon became evident to the English government that it must either give up the contest with America or strengthen its armies. The population of the colonies was generally estimated at three millions. To reduce these three millions to obedience, England had only fifteen thousand men in arms between Nova Scotia and Florida ; allowing all that could be claimed for the difference between well-armed and well-disciplined men and an undisciplined and imperfectly armed militia, it was still easy to see that in a protracted contest, such as this was sure to be, numbers must prevail. Her own subjects England could not fully count upon for filling the ranks, for by many of them the war was disliked from the beginning. The city of London itself was notoriously opposed to it. It was necessary, therefore, for the ministry to cast about them for a man-market from whence to draw their supplies. The first that presented itself to their minds was Russia. The two sovereigns were upon the friendliest terms. England had virtually consented to the partition of Poland, in 1772. The treaty of Kutschuk-Kainardsche, in 1774, had left Russia with a powerful army. What more profitable use could she make of it than by selling it to England for so many guineas a head ? Gunning, the English minister to the Russian court, was instructed to begin negotiations for twenty thousand men : for it was not mere auxiliaries but an army that England sought to bring into the field, thus crushing the insurrection by a well-directed blow. In an interview with Count Panin, Catherine's prime minister, the British envoy asked, as if in casual conversation, whether, if the present measures for the suppression of the insurrection should fail, and his master should find himself under the necessity of calling in foreign troops, he could count upon a body of Russian infantry ? The trained diplomat made no answer, but referred the question to the empress, who, replying in terms of general politeness, professed to feel herself under great obligations to George, which she would gladly repay in the manner most agreeable to him. Without waiting to weigh these words, which in diplomacy might mean much or might mean nothing, Gunning wrote to his court, in all haste, that the empress would furnish the twenty thousand infantry. The important tidings were received by the British court with delight. The commanders serving in America were told on what powerful succor they might rely, and the king in his rapture wrote with his own hand a letter of thanks to his royal sister. Gunning was ordered to push on the negotiations, and, as if he had never known before how little faith can

be placed in the language of diplomacy, was over-
whelmed with astonishment when he was coolly
told that the words of the empress were but the
general expression of a friendly feeling, and that
she had said nothing of the Russian infantry.
Great was the indignation of the English king,
not that the negotiation had failed, but that the
empress had answered his royal autograph by
the hand of a private secretary.

Holland came next, and on a superficial view
the relations between the two countries seemed
to justify the application. But it was met by an
opposition which found an eloquent expositor in
a nobleman of Oberyssel, the Baron van der Ca-
pellen, who, speaking boldly in the name of freedom and national honor, and setting the question
of succor in its true light, succeeded in awakening his countrymen — themselves the descendants
of rebels — to a sense of what they owed to the
memory of their fathers and the cause of freedom.

But there was a country where the name of
freedom was not known, whose nationality was
lost in small principalities and dukedoms, whose
vast resources were sacrificed to the luxury and
vanity of petty sovereigns, each ambitious of
aping on his little stage the splendid corruption
of the French court; yet having strong arms
and hardy bodies to sell, and caring only for the

price that could be extorted for them. To Germany, then, England turned in her need, and her prayer was heard.

There was one part of Germany of which England could freely dispose. George III. was not only King of England, but Elector of Hanover, and as elector could send his Hanoverian troops wherever he saw fit. The garrisons of Gibraltar and Minorca were English. By recalling these and putting Hanoverians, in their place, five well-trained battalions of infantry, amounting in all to two thousand three hundred and sixty-five men, were secured for service against the colonies. In vain did the parliamentary opposition appeal to the bill of rights, and deny the king's right to introduce foreign troops into the kingdom in time of peace. They were told that Minorca and Gibraltar were not parts, but merely dependencies, of the kingdom, and that the American insurrection constituted a state of war. The debate was long and bitter, but the decisive vote of two hundred and three to eighty-one in the Commons, and seventy-five to thirty-two in the Lords, showed how much the partisans of government exceeded the friends of the colonists in number.

No sooner was England's intention to raise troops in Germany known, than officers of all grades, who had been thrown out of service by the close of the Seven Years' War, and the consequent reduction of the armies for which it had found employment, came crowding with proposals to open recruiting offices and raise men. How men were raised has already been told. George, in spite of his royal convictions, felt a humane scruple. "To give German officers authority to raise recruits for me is, in plain English, neither more nor less than to become a man-stealer, which I cannot look upon as a very honorable occupation." But royal scruples seldom go far in the interest of humanity. Recruiting officers with full permission to steal men were soon busily at work in the name of the King of England. Busiest and chief amongst them were the German princes, who had found this a very profitable branch of commerce in former times, and were as much in want of English guineas as England was in want of German soldiers.

There was no time to lose. If the campaign of 1776 was to open with vigor, reinforcements must be speedily on their way. Sir Joseph Yorke, an experienced diplomatist familiar with the ground, was instructed in the summer of 1775 to ascertain on what terms and in what numbers men could be obtained. In September he replied that Hesse-Cassel, Hesse-Darmstadt, Würtemberg, Saxe-Gotha, and Baden were ready to furnish any number of troops at a given time and for a fair price. The Crown Prince of Hesse-

Cassel, in particular, was very earnest to strike a bargain, and close upon his heels came the Prince of Waldeck. Their own letters, mostly in bad French, remain to this day in the English archives, to bear witness to their degradation. I will give a specimen of their English, which is every way worthy of their French.

"My Lord" (writes the Hereditary Prince of Hesse to Lord Suffolk), "the luck I have had to be able to show in some manner my utmost respect and gratitude to the best of kings, by offering my troops to his majesty's service, gives me a very agreeable opportunity of thanking you, my lord, for all your kindness and friendship to me upon that occasion, and begging your pardon for all the trouble I may have provided you in this regard.

"My only wishes are that all the officers and soldiers of my regiment now to his majesty's orders may be animated of the same respectful attachment and utmost zeal I shall ever bear for the king, my generous protector and magnanimous support. May the end they shall fight for answer to the king's upper contentment, and your laudable endeavors, my lord, be granted by the most happiest issue. The continuation of your friendship to me, sir, which I desire very much, assures your goodness and protection to my troops.   I ask in their name this favor from you, and hope you will deserve it.

"Excuse me, sir, if I am not strong enough in the English language for to explain as I should the utmost consideration, and sincere esteem, with which I am forever, my lord, your most humble and very obedient servant,

"WILLIAM, H. P. OF HESSE."

The most important among these petty princes was the Duke of Brunswick, who paid thirty thousand thalers a year to the director of his opera and purveyor of his pleasures, and three hundred to his librarian, the great Lessing.   His little territory of about sixty square miles had a population of one hundred and fifty thousand souls, and an income of a million and a half.   His debts amounted to nearly twelve millions.   A lover of pomp, capricious and reckless in his expenditure, he had been compelled to admit his son, the crown prince, to a partnership of authority, making the signatures of both essential to the validity of a document.   Fortunately for the duke's creditors, the son was as parsimonious as the father was extravagant, and let no opportunity of raising money escape him.   Such was the condition of the court of Brunswick when England sent Colonel William Fawcitt to ask for troops.

Had the English envoy been as well versed in the higher as in the lower arts of diplomacy, he would have obtained all that he asked without modification or delay. But, ignorant of the straits to which the duke was reduced for want of money, he began by asking for what he might have commanded, and involving himself in negotiations where a few firm words would have brought both father and son to his feet. The crown prince was not slow to turn to account the advantage which the slow-witted Englishman had given him, and using artfully and skillfully the name and coequal authority of his father, presently gained virtual control of the negotiation, which in itself was little more than a higgling over details. Fawcitt boasts of the perseverance with which he has beat down the German's prices, and the persistence with which he has resisted some of his claims. The main object of the transaction was won, England got her soldiers, — four thousand infantry and three hundred light dragoons, — Brunswick her money, her duke and minister their special pickings, and the English envoy a diamond ring worth one hundred pounds as a reward for his good offices.

The first division was to start at once for the seat of war. On examination by the British commissioner, it was found to contain too many old men. The duke's zeal for the king's service did not prevent him from palming off upon him men altogether unfit to bear arms. "The front and rear," wrote Fawcitt to Lord Suffolk, "are composed of sound and strong men, but the centre is worthless. It is composed of raw recruits, who not only are too small, but also imperfectly grown, and in part too young." Nor did the trickery end here. This same duke, who lived surrounded by expensive mistresses, sent off his soldiers upon a late spring voyage with uniforms unfit for service, and no overcoats or cloaks. It was not till they got to Portsmouth that they obtained their first supply of shoes and stockings. Their commander, Baron Riedesel, was compelled to borrow five thousand pounds from the English government in order to procure for his starving and freezing men the simplest articles of necessity.

Thus far they had had the rapacity of their own sovereign to contend with. They now came into contact with the rapacity of English tradesmen. When they got to sea and opened the boxes of dragoon shoes, they found them to be thin ladies' shoes, utterly unfit for the purpose for which they were designed. Such are some of the fruits of that great demoralizer — war. We need not go far back for the parallel.

Towards the end of May the second division was mustered into service. They were nearly all

recruits, levied especially for service in America ;
many of them, as in the first, too old or too
young, or imperfectly grown and too feeble to
carry a musket.   But the blame called forth by
the condition of the first division was not altogether vain, and the arms and uniforms were
good.   The officers did not escape without their
share of suffering.   The cabins were so small
that their occupants were compelled to lie on one
another in heaps.   The Bristol merchants, who
had supplied the transports with bedding, had
made the most of their bargain.   The pillows
were five inches long and seven broad, the size
of a common pincushion ; and the mattresses so
thin that with a coarse woolen blanket and cov-
erlid they hardly weighed seven pounds.   The
food was prepared upon the same honest scale.
The ham was worm-eaten, the water dirty, and
the ship's stores had been ripened by lying in the
English magazines ever since the Seven Years'
War.   Thus the powerful King of England and
the petty sovereigns of Germany leagued together to buy and sell the blood of the unprotected German peasant.

Let us carry this study a little further.   Elated
with the success of his first negotiation, Fawcitt
turned his face towards Hesse-Cassel.   Germany
" was all before him where to choose," and he
chose, or rather Lord Suffolk chose for him, the

brilliant court of Hesse-Cassel for the next scene of his labors. The Duke of Hesse-Cassel, like his brother of Brunswick, felt no Christian scruples, no humane misgivings, no paternal doubts about trafficking in the blood of his subjects. Landgrave Charles I. had set the example, and his successors had followed it. He let out his soldiers to Venice, and it might have been accepted as a mitigation of his crime that it was to serve against the Turks, the deadly enemies of Christian civilization. But it was not to the Venetians as the defenders of Christianity that he let them, but as the best paymasters in the market. From 1687, when Charles I. sent one thousand men to fight for the Venetians, till the end of the Seven Years' War, Hessians were found in one or the other of the contending armies, and always among the best disciplined and bravest of its soldiers. With the proceeds of their blood Charles I. built barracks and churches, constructed the water-works of the Weissenstein, and set up the statue of Hercules. His successors followed close in his footsteps, holding at one time twenty-four thousand men under arms, and always commanding the highest prices for their blood. Marble palaces, galleries rich with paintings and statues, spacious villas, and all the luxuries of the most advanced civilization bore witness to the wealth of the sovereign ; their homes,

13

and the boys, old men and women doing the work of ripe manhood, attested the oppression of the subject. There was a deep-set melancholy on the faces of the women. "When we are dead we are done with it," was a common saying with the men. When a father asked for his son, whom the conscription had torn from him, he was sent to the mines. If a mother besought that he to whom she had looked for the support of her age might be restored to her, she was sent to the workhouse. Some of the barbarous punishments by which soldiers were terrified into obedience were inflicted in the streets. "Never," says Weber, in his "Travels of a German in Germany," "did I see so many poor wretches chased through the streets as in Cassel. It is less injurious to the health than running the gauntlet," the officers told him; and well it might be, for that gauntlet was run through a narrow lane of men, each provided with a stout cane and bound to apply it with full force to the backs of the delinquents. In cases of desertion, the greatest of crimes, the offender was made to run this gauntlet two days in succession, and twelve times each day. Can we wonder that the terrible punishment often ended in death?

The poet tells us that —

> Ingenuas didicisse fideliter artes
> Emollit mores nec sinit esse feros.

I could wish that this were always true, but I
fear that history will not bear us out in the belief.　Landgrave Frederick II., whose reign from
1760 to 1785 covers the whole period in which
we are most interested, can hardly be regarded
as an illustration of the rule.　His mixed character will repay a more attentive study.

He had inherited from his father a territory of
one hundred and fifty-six German square miles,
with a population of three hundred thousand
souls.　Over this population he exercised an absolute control, and by his wealth, his connec-
tions, and the favorable position of his territories,
he was counted among the most powerful of his
brother princes.　From his ancestors he inherited business talent, indiscreet selfishness, coarse
sensuality, and obstinate self-will.　He had found
Protestantism too rigorous, and became a Catholic in order to enjoy greater religious freedom,
though he was not only indifferent to religion,
but prided himself on playing the part of an il-
luminato, a protector of the arts and sciences,
and a correspondent of Voltaire.　He founded
schools of a higher order, and even made some
humane laws; but his culture was all on the sur-
face, and his life was defiled by an indecent lib-
ertinism.　French manners, French literature,
and, above all, French licentiousness, reigned at
his court, and to form some idea of its corrupting

power we have only to remember that at the beginning of his career he was a contemporary of
Louis XV. If he spent freely upon churches
and museums, he spent more freely for the grati-
fication of his voluptuousness. Yet with all this
love of pleasure and display, he left at his death
sixty million thalers in ready money. Where
did he get it? A skillfully managed lottery furnished part; but the traffic in soldiers the greater
part.

For him also the American war was a godsend,
awakening new hopes for himself, and, as with
his brother princes, new zeal and grateful attachment to "the best of kings." We have seen
how Fawcitt had been outwitted in his negotiations with the prime minister of Brunswick. He
was still less able to cope with Von Schlieffen,
the prime minister of Hesse-Cassel, — a man of
both military and civil experience, a skillful negotiator, profoundly versed in the practical study
of human nature, and thoroughly familiar with
the aims and wishes of his sovereign. Fortunately for that sovereign, his minister was en-
tirely devoted to his interests.

The negotiation began by a master stroke,
which represented the landgrave as sensitive and
nervous, and therefore in a state of mind that required delicate management. The English envoy bit eagerly at the bait, and made no secret of

the dependence of his sovereign upon foreign aid. " How many men does he want ? " was the first question. From ten thousand to twelve thousand, answered Fawcitt, little dreaming that the small state could furnish so many. He was told that the Hessian troops were on the best footing, and the king could have all that he asked for. Fawcitt was very happy, for the main object of his mission seemed secure. The troops promised, all the rest was merely a discussion of details. But in the skillful diplomacy of his opponent these details became concessions, cunningly interwoven, and leading by subtle interpretations from one admission to another. First came a claim for hospital expenses during the last war, — a claim the envoy had never heard of before, and concerning which he was therefore obliged to write home for instructions.

Meanwhile he urged on the preparation of the contract, which, to the wonder of diplomatists and the disgust of thoughtful Englishmen, took the form, not of a convention for hiring soldiers, as in the case of Brunswick, but of a treaty on equal terms between the mistress of the seas and a petty German landgrave, as high contracting powers. We need not, however, look far for the cause of the unwonted pliability of the English government. The margrave had money, and could wait. The king had no troops, and could not wait.

I will not follow the details of this negotiation any further. Both parties obtained their
object. England got the men; the landgrave
got his money. The time for the embarkation
was fixed, and when it came, the first division
of 8397 was mustered into the English service
by Fawcitt, who seemed at a loss for words to express his admiration of their soldierly appearance.
On the 12th of August, 1776, they entered New
York Bay. On the 27th they took a brilliant
part, under De Heister, in the battle of Long
Island. A gale of wind, a persistent calm, any
of the common chances of the ocean, and they
would have been too late, and Howe would not
have dared to fight the battle which won him his
knighthood; Washington would have had time
to strengthen his works on both islands; Greene,
who of all the American officers was the only one
perfectly familiar with the ground, would have
recovered sufficiently from his untimely fever to
resume his command, and the whole aspect of the
campaign of 1776 would have been altered. So
much, in great enterprises, often depends upon
a happy concurrence of incidents. Henceforth
let it be borne in mind that in every battle of
the war of independence, hired men of Germany
play an important part.

On the 2d of June the second division was
mustered into service. On the 18th of October

it landed at New Rochelle. It consisted of 3997 men, not the trained men of well-knit sinews who formed the first division, but chiefly young men of seventeen or eighteen, who had been raised to serve in America. As general of division we find Knyphausen, whose name soon became familiar to both armies. Among the colonels of the first division we find Rahl, who commanded at Trenton when Washington came upon it by surprise in the cold gray of a morning after Christmas ; and Donop, who fell mortally wounded, as he led his men to the attack of Redbank, and died exclaiming, " I die the victim of my own ambition and the avarice of my sovereign." Did those bitter words ever reach the ears of that sovereign ? Not if we may judge by the cold, business-like method with which he bargained that three wounded men should count as one killed, and one killed as one newly levied, or thirty crowns banco.

But this second division was not so easily raised as the first. The alarm had spread rapidly among a people still suffering from the wounds of the Seven Years' War. The only refuge was desertion, and although the frontiers were closely guarded, deserters passed daily into the neighboring territories, where, from the people at least, they found a ready reception. To check this the king, as Elector of Hanover, put forth all his authority to restore these poor wretches to their sovereign ; and the sovereign, to prove his paternal tenderness, reduced the war taxes by half; taking good care to secure for himself an ample compensation from England. "The treasury," to borrow the energetic language of a German historian, "was filled with blood and tears." Yet in spite of all the efforts both of the king and the landgrave, the desertion continued; the difficulty of finding recruits increased ; native Hessians able to bear arms disappeared from the towns and fields ; and it was only by stealing men wherever they could be found that the landgrave could fulfill his promises. Meanwhile he went to Italy to enjoy his money and form new plans of embellishment.

From Cassel Fawcitt hastened to Hanau, where he found the Crown Prince of Hesse-Cassel, and, following up his negotiations, had a new convention all ready in the course of the first twenty-four hours. He was delighted with the "impetuous zeal" of the prince. But the difficulty of his task was increasing ; not from any hesitation on the part of the sovereign, who thought only of his gains, but because the subject had conceived a strong aversion for service beyond the sea. Excellent soldiers as the Germans were, they shrank with repugnance and terror from a voyage across the Atlantic. Those of my readers who have walked through a steerage crowded with emigrants will readily conceive what the sufferings of those poor soldiers must have been, badly fed, badly lodged, and worse than crowded. Draw the picture as you may, you cannot color it too highly. Little thought did either the king or the prince take of this. Each had his immediate object, and cared little for anything besides.

The Waldeckers came next; and Fawcitt pressing them on through new difficulties, they were ready in November to take a decided part in the assault of Fort Washington. For they fought gallantly, it will be remembered, on the north side, where both attack and defense were bloodiest and hottest. German writers tell us how the wounded cursed and swore, bewailing their lot; but if the prince was to be trusted, they only "longed for an opportunity to sacrifice themselves for the best of kings."

The avarice of the German princes grew with success. All longed to come in for a share of this abundant harvest. Bavaria asked to put in her little sickle, but was refused. England might have raised her tone, for every applicant wrote as if all Germany were at her feet. But in truth the aversion to the service grew daily, and the difficulty of conveying troops to the place of muster caused serious embarrassments, which if En-

gland had been less in need might have led to
the renunciation of the contract. But as has been
already said, England wanted men and the princes
wanted money, and thus the evil work went on,
till there were no longer men to be bought or stolen.

There is a painful monotony in this story of inhumanity and crime, of the avarice of money and
the avarice of power. It is common to speak of
George III. as a man of a narrow mind but of
an excellent heart ; a moral king while so many
of his contemporary kings disgraced the thrones
on which they sat. This is too light a view of
so grave a subject. Superiority of power carries
with it superiority of moral obligation, and the
man from whose will good or evil flows, compel-
ling millions to go with it, must be held to a
sterner reckoning than his fellow-men. Let us
not pass lightly over this grave subject. The
balancing of responsibilities, the just meting out
of judgment to the strong and to the weak, is one
of the most serious duties of the historian. The
man who accepts a post of responsibility is bound
to do whatever this responsibility imposes. Weigh
the British king in this balance and grievously
will he be found wanting.

And what shall we say of the German princes ?
Their lives speak for them. The pervading character of their relations to their subjects was cold-
hearted selfishness, a wanton sacrifice of the labor

and lives of their subjects to their own caprice and pleasure. Compare their spacious palaces with the comfortless cottages of the peasant; their sumptuous tables, covered with the delicate inventions of French cookery, with the coarse bread, almost the peasant's only meal; see their splendid theatres, maintained by taxes that rob the laborer of half the fruits of his toil; see how desolate the fields look, how deserted the highways, how silent the streets; see what sadness sits upon the brows of the women, what despair on the faces of the men; and think what manner of man he must be who reigns over subjects like these!

It has been said that the convention with the crown prince at Hanau was discussed and signed in twenty-four hours. The Prince of Waldeck followed, and soon the name of Waldeckers — first written in blood on the northern ridge of Fort Washington — became a name of fear and hatred to Americans. It would be useless — disgusting, rather — to dwell upon the monotonous record of this buying and selling of human blood. I will give a few incidents only to complete the picture.

A spirit of rivalry had grown up among these dukes and landgraves and princes, such rivalry as only avarice could awaken. They crowded around Fawcitt, and, while protesting that devotion to the majesty of England was their only motive, took good care to drive keen bargains and insist upon the uttermost farthing. They intrigued against each other in all the tortuous ways familiar to petty princes, bringing even religion to their aid, reminding Fawcitt how dangerous an element so large a proportion of Catholics would be in an English army. England wanted an army of twenty thousand men, with which she hoped to bring the war to a close in the course of another year; for till the Christmas of 1776 the campaign had gone all in her favor, and her hired troops had borne themselves bravely. She might have spoken in a more commanding tone. But the surprise of Trenton had thrown nearly nine hundred of these valiant mercenaries into the hands of the Americans and changed the whole aspect of the war. New troops were more needed than ever. She was again obliged to ask urgently and accept the hardest conditions.

The American service was now better understood, but not better liked. The Margrave of Anspach encountered serious obstacles in sending his troops to the place of embarkation. At Ochsenfurt they revolted and refused to embark. A skillful leader might have opposed a formidable resistance, but their officers were not with them in heart, and information of the untoward event was immediately sent to the margrave. He instantly mounted his horse, not stopping long enough to take a change of linen or even his watch, and, followed by only two or three attendants, rode at full speed to the scene of the revolt. At the sight of their master the hearts of these bold men, so daring in the face of the enemy, misgave them, and they penitently returned to their allegiance.

Other difficulties awaited other corps on their march. The electors of Mainz and Trier stopped them as they passed through their territories, and claimed some of them as deserters. At Coblentz seventeen Hessians were taken out of the boats at the suggestion of the imperial minister, Metternich. Another element of dissension was introduced, and deep menaces were uttered for the insult to the Hessian flag. But this, also, was presently forgotten; the work went on, and the new band of mercenaries reached New York in safety.

Among the mistakes of the English government, the greatest, perhaps, of all was the failure to understand the spirit and resources of the colonies, and the consequent prolongation of the war. The surprise of Trenton was, both by the actual loss of men and the still more fatal loss of prestige, a heavy blow. The privation of such troops under such circumstances imposed the necessity of immediate reinforcements. The only

market in which they could be found was Germany, and that market was nearly drained. But
as long as a man was to be had; his sovereign
was eager to sell him and England to buy.

As early as December, 1776, the Duke of Würtemberg had offered four thousand men, and
Fawcitt had been instructed to enter into negotiations with him. But upon a closer examination
it was found that he was bankrupt. He had no
arms and no uniforms. To prevent the men from
deserting they were kept without pay. The
officers' tents had been cut up to eke out the dec-
orations of the duke's rural festivals. The prospect was gloomy. Sir Joseph Yorke was called
into council, but he had no new market to recommend. Saxe-Gotha and Darmstadt might furnish
a few. The Prince of Anhalt-Zerbst was willing
to furnish two battalions. He was a brother of
Catherine II., and a hearty hater of the great
Frederick. His territories were wretchedly poor.
His eagerness to get money embarrassed his negotiations, which were broken off by Suffolk, but
resumed in the autumn of 1777 on the recommendation of Sir Joseph Yorke. But England
wanted more men. Then adventurers began to
come forward with propositions more or less fea-
sible, but all aiming at the fathomless purse of
England. A Baron Eichberg offered to open a
recruiting office in Minorca; then a regiment of

Sclavonians, who were also good sailors, and after the war were to found a colony for holding the Americans in check. The offer was not accepted. Other offers were made, but by impoverished men, who, when the time came, failed to meet their engagements. And thus was it till the end of the war ; the only contracts that held were the first six : the contracts, namely, with Brunswick, Cassel, Hanau, Waldeck, Anspach, and Zerbst. The history of these six contracts covers the whole ground to the spring of 1777, when the difficulty of finding recruits increased. All that follows is in the main but a repetition of the original nego-tiations. For a year the disgraceful work pros-pered. But early in 1777 the market was nearly drained, and though new engagements continued to be made, they were seldom fulfilled. The story was still sad and humiliating ; I shall follow its details no further.[1] Here I must pause a mo-ment to call attention to the heartless betrayal of his own soldiers by the Duke of Brunswick. Two thousand of these wretches had been made pris-oners at Saratoga ; and the duke, fearing that to exchange them would interfere with his profit and diffuse a general dissatisfaction with the service, when so many witnesses against it were scattered

---

[1] The reader who wishes to study this subject more fully should read *Der Soldatenhandel deutscher Fürsten nach Amerika* (1775 bis 1783), von Friedrich Kapp, Berlin, 1864.

through the country, urged the English government to delay their exchange till the war was ended.

Frederick of Prussia and the emperor were opposed to the selling of men for foreign service; not from any feeling for the misery which it caused, but because their own political horizon was overcast and they might soon need them for their own service. It has been said that Frederick was moved by sentiments of humanity, and that with a bitter practical satire he imposed the same tax upon the passage of these men through his territories that he had been accustomed to impose upon cattle. But we have very little reason to count humanity among Frederick's virtues. He hated England for her desertion of him when Bute became minister and Chatham was forced to retire. In November, 1777, he refused the Anspachers and Hanauers a passage through his territories; sorely embarrassing the German sovereigns and their English customers. They knew not which way to turn. If they should attempt to pass through Holland and the Netherlands, the discontented and ill-provided men would desert by hundreds. When at last the march began, three hundred and thirty-four men did desert in ten days. The disgraceful drama closed in 1778 with the embarkation of the levies of the Prince of Zerbst. And thus Frederick was our involuntary ally.

There was another ordeal to pass before the bargain was brought to a close. Would Parliament approve this degradation? The debates were long and bitter, and brought out the thinkers and orators of both houses. In the Commons, Burke characterized the bargain as shameful and dear. In the Lords, Camden branded it as a sale of cattle for the shambles. Even the butcher of Culloden condemned it as an attempt to suppress constitutional liberty in America. But the ministry prevailed by large majorities in both houses. England had not yet opened her eyes to the inhumanity and bad statesmanship of the war.

But England was not alone. The moral sense of Europe had not yet awakened. The old spirit of feudalism had not yet lost its hold upon the nobles nor upon the people. The noble still felt that the commoner was infinitely below him. The commoner and day-laborer could not but believe that the noble was really far above them. A few voices were raised in the defense of human rights. The most powerful of these in France was the voice of Mirabeau, who, though a noble himself, had also been the victim of tyranny. And in Germany it is pleasant to find Schiller on the side of humanity, stigmatizing the trade in men in his " Kabale und Liebe ; " while the great Kant went still further, and embraced the cause of the American colonists with all the energy of

14

his vast intellect. Klopstock and Lessing spoke in low tones, and we listen in vain for the voice of Goethe.

It is impossible to give with perfect accuracy the numbers of the Germans employed by England in this fatal war. The English archives contain one part of the story, and that the most important — the numbers actually mustered into service. But the various German archives, which contain the record of all who were put on the rolls, are not all accessible to the historical inquirer. This part of the subject has been carefully studied by Schlozer, and the result compared by Mr. Kapp with the statements in the English state paper office. Mr. Kapp's figures are as follows : —

	No. Men furnished.	No. returned home.
Brunswick	5,723	2,708
Hesse-Cassel	16,992	10,492
Hesse-Hanau	2,422	1,441
Waldeck	1,225	505
Anspach	1,644	1,183
Anhalt-Zerbst	1,160	984
Total	29,166	17,313

Thus the total loss was 11,853.

It is difficult to establish with certainty the sums which this army of foreigners took from the tax-payers of England. Strongly supported as they were in Parliament, ministers did not dare to tell the whole story openly, but put many things under false titles. They did not dare frankly to say, Every man that is killed puts so many thalers into the sovereign's pocket, every three wounded men count for one dead man. Even the Parliament of Lord North might have shrunk from the contemplation of figures thus stained with tears and blood. As near as it can be established by a careful comparison of the English authorities, the sums paid under various names by the English treasury amounted in round numbers to seven million pounds sterling, or, at the present standard, fourteen million pounds sterling. Had these fourteen millions been used for the good of the people by whose sweat and blood they were won, we might still find some grounds for consolation in the reflection that the good thus done to one would, by a common law of humanity, sooner or later extend to all. But this fruit of the blood of the people went to satisfy the vain ambitions of display and the unbounded sensuality of the sovereign. Men whose names might have stood high in the annals of war, if they had fought for their country, are known in history as fighters for hire.

Lightning Source UK Ltd.
Milton Keynes UK
UKHW020642090223
416652UK00001B/138